St. Louis Community College

Forest Park
Florissant Valley
Meramec

Instructional Resources
St. Louis, Missouri

VICTIMS OF
SOVIET TERROR

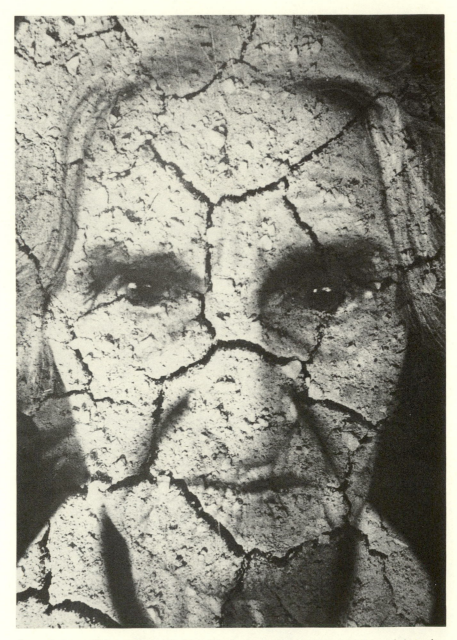

An artistic rendition of the toll of totalitarianism, presented at the Memorial seminar "Maps of the Gulag" in the Historical Archive Institute, Moscow, April 19, 1990.

Victims of Soviet Terror

The Story of the Memorial Movement

NANCI ADLER

Foreword by JONATHAN SANDERS

PRAEGER

Westport, Connecticut
London

Library of Congress Cataloging-in-Publication Data

Adler, Nanci.
    Victims of Soviet terror : the story of the Memorial movement /
Nanci Adler ; foreword by Jonathan Sanders.
       p.   cm.
    Includes bibliographical references (p.   ) and index.
    ISBN 0-275-94502-2 (alk. paper)
    1. Vsesoiuznoe istoriko-prosvetitel'skoe obshchestvo "Memorial."
2. Soviet Union—History. 3. Political persecution—Soviet Union—
History. I. Title.
DK266.3.A585   1993
947.084—dc20   92-46164

British Library Cataloguing in Publication Data is available.

Library of Congress Catalog Card Number: 92-46164
ISBN: 0-275-94502-2

First published in 1993

Praeger Publishers, 88 Post Road West, Westport, CT 06881
An imprint of Greenwood Publishing Group, Inc.

Printed in the United States of America

∞™

The paper used in this book complies with the
Permanent Paper Standard issued by the National
Information Standards Organization (Z39.48-1984).

10 9 8 7 6 5 4 3 2 1

Copyright Acknowledgment

The author and publisher gratefully acknowledge permission to reprint the following
copyright material:

Yevgeny Yevtushenko, "The Heirs to Stalin," *The Current Digest of the Soviet Press* 14,
no. 40 (1962): 5. Translation copyright 1962 by *The Current Digest of the Soviet Press*,
published weekly at Columbus, Ohio. Reprinted by permission of the *Digest*.

Dedicated to Rob
for being here and there and everywhere

Contents

Foreword

Candles and silence drove a stake into the heart of Soviet conformity during the early evening of October 30, 1989. Individual Soviet citizens encircled KGB headquarters at Dzerzhinsky (now Lubyanka) Square. They formed a human chain around the office building of repression and its 200-cell prison. Fear once impelled people to cross Moscow streets to avoid even the shadow cast by this dreaded citadel. But on the last day in October 1989, the International Day of Political Prisoners, perhaps two thousand men and women bravely surrounded the real center of the empire that made Soviet life evil. The All-Union Society Memorial inspired and organized the encirclement.

Images generated at Dzerzhinsky Square soon captured worldwide attention. Removal of the statue honoring secret police founder Felix Dzerzhinsky (1877–1926) became *the* iconographic device, *the* visual metaphor for the Soviet regime's collapse following the aborted putsch of August 1991. After decades of sameness, stagnation, change's rapid swirls are remembered as conflated. It seems an age between the shocking demonstration of October 1989 and the three days that shook the world of August 1991. To Muscovites it feels like two ages between the initial, semi-clandestine meetings of the group that would become Memorial in August 1987 and the free, democratic Russia that emerged after the death of the Soviet Union's last great Stalinist, Lazar Moiseyevich Kaganovich (1893–1991), when the reactionary coup of his heirs failed.[1]

Never mind that in the frantic rush of events, such as October 30, 1990, when thousands took to the streets around Lubyanka, Memorial buried more of the lingering fear. That night a loudspeaker truck blurted out those long-hidden facts—the names and deadly sentences pronounced on individuals who had disappeared in Stalin's Gulag. The crowd gathered in a little park opposite the main Lubyanka KGB building. There, Father Gleb Yakunin, a priest jailed under Brezhnev (elected a People's Deputy under Gorbachev) and Oleg Volkov, one man sentenced to the Gulag under Stalin who survived twenty-eight years of incarceration, unveiled a stone memorial brought from the Solovetsky Island labor camp. Almost unnoticed in the crowd stood an old woman wrapped in a beige and green wool hat and black and white scarf. She had survived the Gulag, survived the transition from membership in the Bolshevik elite to outcast as a relative of an enemy of the people. Anna Mikhailovna Larina, widow of Nikolai Bukharin, the victim of Stalin's last great show trial, the model for Arthur Koestler's protagonist in *Darkness at Noon*, quietly observed the October 1990 rites of collective atonement and truth telling.

Only those who knew Anna Mikhailovna recognized her as a poignant symbol. The ceremonies had no celebrities; everyone was equal in the ranks of Stalin's victims. It was the democratic equality of the Gulag camps brought to Moscow's streets. It was the democratic impulse of the event's organizers.

This evening, too, was organized by the All-Union Society Memorial. Still, the first public encircling of Lubyanka one year earlier provides the key to Memorial's power, accomplishments, and significance. Memorial did not philosophize about the need to fill in the blank spots in Soviet history; it acted. Memorial did not simply mourn those who perished; it organized. It carefully planned the stunning October 1989 event at Lubyanka that attracted worldwide attention.

Young and old encircled Lubyanka, remembering those who had perished. One woman held a black and white picture of her father. She explained that many people came to remember their people who had perished, "I'm bearing witness against the murder of my father who disappeared into the depth of Stalin's killing machine in 1937." Her name was Sophie. Sophie was not a dissident, not a political activist in the usual sense of the term. Tears filled her eyes, but her voice never quavered. "Today is the memorial day for political prisoners," she explained. "This is the first time I've observed this day. Before I was afraid, before I did not know of this day, before my father's disappearance and death was simply one of the millions of personal and family tragedies generated by the Gulag system."

For those like Sophie and those learning lessons from all the Sophies, the personal had become political. They bore witness to truths suppressed, to realities denied. This was not an obscurant or antiquarian movement. Protest was inherent in the action. Most overtly, a few carried signs demanding "defense of democratic deputies," the progessive few squeezing into public life through political openings created by Communist Party General Secretary Mikhail Sergeyevich Gorbachev.

More inherently, the human chain represented the movement from below to create a civil society. In essence this was a Gandhian phenomenon. It followed the footsteps of Mohandas Karamchand Gandhi not so much in the sense of being nonviolent, although it was inherently nonviolent and anti-violence; rather, it embodied the values in Satyagraha. Gandhi coined the term meaning "holding on to the truth" and hence (as he wrote in 1922) "force of righteousness."

Marshalling the forces of righteousness, sending them into battle against the Soviet establishment, is an appropriate response to adversity by the intelligentsia. That peculiarly Russian body, the intelligentsia, thrived for over two centuries on a commitment to the power of ideas. Its roots are best described by Marc Raeff in *The Origins of the Russian Intelligentsia*; its moral vision is embodied in the person of Soviet Russia's secular saint, Andrei Sakharov.

For more than twenty years the Nobel Peace Prize winner stood as the country's moral center. Until his death in December 1989, Sakharov pushed to overcome the atomization of human existence. His own example became a force for change. His contrariness was intellectual—he wrote books and tracts; organizational—he helped gather under one human rights umbrella disparate groupings of contrarians; demonstrational—he publicly protested authoritarian acts large and small. Sakharov's moral conscience and sense of social responsibility was viewed like a seedling breaking though the cement of a city pavement with its vital force.[2] The same could be said for Memorial and the role it played as the foremost informal organization fomenting what became the self-liberation of Soviet society.

The deliberate arbitrariness of rule, the deadly purges, the Orwellian propaganda were all essential elements in the scheme Hannah Arendt identified as totalitarianism. Though never total, in its Soviet variant this oppresive authoritarianism divided each person from the other. It fostered a fragmented society based on universal suspicion. Bearing witness to truth and universal moral values, Sakharov showed Soviet citizens how to break through the loneliness, the collective alienation that had become life's norm. He always spoke out, whether it was convenient or not, whether it was politically correct or not. "Inside myself," Sakharov once explained, "I have always felt free." Memorial sought to replicate that sense of freedom for everyone inside the Soviet Union. It acted to make the free individual the rule, not the extraordinary exception in a highly authoritarian and arbitrary society.

On that crisp October night in 1989 it was not Sakharov but the bellwether of liberal intelligentsia activism, poet Yevgeny Yevtushenko, who provided perspective. The silent vigil bore witness to the most unspeakably horrible chapters in Soviet history. Yevtushenko acknowledged: "It is an evening of hope. I see here some old people, some very young people; some intellectuals, some workers; some people from provincial cities and towns; Soviet citizens of all classes. That unity gives me hope." The event's historical significance struck Yevtushenko as well: "It is absolutely unbelievable," he said, "three or four years ago even it was absolutely impossible. Impossible. The crowds, the candles . . . all of it around the KGB. And this is an officially sanctioned meeting."

Yevtushenko did not explain it was Memorial, the organization in which he played a key role, that made the impossible, possible. Rather, he emphasized the transformational force of the idea of "memory." Remembering the real past, remembering the real legacy of Soviet power instead of its propaganda claims, satisfying the thirst for historical truth was a way of taking moral responsibility for the heritage of Stalinism and undoing it.

More than simply reclaiming history, Memorial harnessed what one of its founders, Yuri Afanasyev, called "the energy of historical knowledge." Memorial became a seedbed of activism. It brought together the incoherent elements to which Yevtushenko alluded. It brought them into a nascent united front against Soviet continuities.

The best organized demonstrations—in fact, often the only carefully planned rallies, marches, and public displays of alienation in the Soviet capital—occurred with Memorial's participation. Marshalls from Memorial ensured that surging crowds would not stampede. Memorial often acted as a switchboard in providing reliable information on political activities, sanctioned and unsanctioned, taking place around the country. Memorial helped foster the progressive popular front, "Democratic Russia." With rare grace Memorial provided services and acted as a nurturing seedbed for other organizations, but it withdrew once independent organizations had established themselves.

Memorial put its concerns for moral responsibility at the center of Soviet life, but it resisted putting itself at the center as a be-all and end-all organization. Its activism, intellectual and practical, made possible the swift telescoping of events from Dzerzhinsky Square in October 1989 to the celebratory dismantling of the Dzerzhinsky statue in August 1991.

In *Victims of Soviet Terror: The Story of the Memorial Movement,* Nanci Adler uncovers the history of this remarkable organization from its beginings in 1987 as a quasi-conspiratorial circle—one that clearly manifests its dissident roots—through its remarkable breakthroughs in the kaleidoscopic last year of Soviet power to its triumphal establishment as one of the quiet moral pillars of democratic Russia. Ms. Adler brings to this pioneering study a rare combination of talents. She has the careful researcher's dispassionate discipline, respect for the paper and microform documents.

The eye-witness insight into the human foibles of her subjects—her all-too-human heroes—does not fail her. From the Memorial waiting room, her fly-on-the-wall perspective, as ordinary people make pilgrimages to report, to find out, to gain some understanding of the personal tragedies that have flattened their lives, gives this book real-life dimensions.

Moreover, she brings the deep sensibilities of a humanist as well as a human rights advocate. She is in the best sense of the term a committed scholar.

Adler keeps her sights firmly fixed on contemporary relevance. But she avoids the traps of (the late, but little lamented) Sovietology: obsessive preoccupation with high politics—politics with people, popular psychology, and family histories left out; overemphasis on Moscow as if it is the entire country; debilitating theory envy that substitutes "scientific" theorems of politics (based on the fairy tale assumption that politics is a science) for understanding the art of living or the drama of daily life. Thankfully this study is jargon free.

Nanci Adler writes contemporary history not so much from the bottom or top but from the middle and the side. She knits together the histories of the Russian past that are important for understanding society today. As a phenomenon the Memorial movement, Adler shows, helps us understand how revolution is revelation. In this case the revolutionary movement of Democratic Russia builds by filling in the blank spots in a nation's own understanding of its past, while it is repudiating, renouncing, and remaking that experience.

To provide context and perspective Adler synthesizes one of Soviet history's few chapters already chronicled (and about to be made obsolete by Memorial's work): its Gulag system. She traces the rise of the new Soviet class of Gulag inhabitants with an unusual sensitivity for its labyrinthian character. Perhaps this comes from previous study of Kafka's mental world. The general reader needs to understand well how Stalin's mass terror and the system of forced labor camps served as a building block for Soviet reality. The specialists who know the monographic materials need only be reminded by this synthesis of the centrality to the Soviet experience of the great social mobilization into the Gulag. But both general readers and specialists must avoid replicating the latest Russian passion: validating the ideologically driven categorical declarations of cold war Sovietology. The danger of new myths and new stereotypes replacing the old, on both sides of the Atlantic, remains very real. Memorial lays the groundwork for critically minded students, West and East, to weave together the complex truths that are Soviet history.[3]

Memorial is in the business of building monuments to truth and of truth. Various branches have raised and are raising memorial stones, statues, and plaques to victims of Soviet mass terror. Memorial erects no monuments to itself. Indeed, its modesty, its lack of self-aggrandizement has meant Memorial has faded from Western consciousness now that the riveting spectacles organized at Dzerzhinsky Square have disappeared into contemporary history's netherworld. Memorial's fifteen minutes of global-village fame seemingly vanished before it gained the recognition of an Amnesty International or a Helsinki Watch. Nanci Adler provides the first substantial history, the first scholarly monument to this monumentally significant organization.

Memorial is now officially ensconced in its own solid headquarters building on a quiet Moscow street. Just a stone's throw from the Russian Justice Ministry building, Memorial headquarters is now a beehive of scholarly activity as specialists build data banks, daily adding information to the history of injustices visited upon the Soviet people. Memorial helped topple the omnipotent KGB.

In post-putsch Russia the KGB's successor organization is merely potent. But so far it is powerful enough to keep Memorial from realizing a dream Yevtushenko made public on that October night in 1989—a dream, the poet explained, he had first heard from the Soviet, now American, sculptor Ernst Neizvestny during Brezhnev's years of stagnation: making the KGB building on Dzerzhinsky Square into a museum honoring the human tragedy of Soviet-style "modernization." The doors of the Lubyanka office complex have opened a little. Now documents from the KGB archives swamp the careful Memorial researchers. They may spend the rest of their lives making sense of the official evidence of repression. Meanwhile they continue gathering source material—documents, testimony, and oral histories from victims, their kin, their descendants. Through its work Memorial proves that history is not at its end. Because of the careful investigations by Memorial and Nanci Adler's pioneering study of Memorial itself, Soviet history as well as that of the new democratic Russia is really just beginning.

Dr. Jonathan Sanders, Moscow

NOTES

1. It seems light years away from the "birthday" of the Soviet human rights movement, December 5, 1965, when a few brave souls demonstrated on Moscow's Pushkin Square. They unwrapped a banner proclaiming, "Respect the Soviet Constitution," and the KGB quickly wrapped them up.

2. See Marshall D. Shulman, "The Sakharov Manifesto," *Saturday Review*, November 23, 1968, p. 51.

3. Lenin, who well understood the anti-historical impulses of ideological warriors, put it well: "History generally, and the history of revolutions in particular, is always richer in content, more varied, and more many-sided, more lively and more subtle than those representing the best parties and the most class-conscious spokesman of the advanced classes imagine." (Jonathan Edward Sanders, *The Union of Unions: Political, Economic, Civil and Human Rights Organizations in the 1905 Russian Revolution* [Ann Arbor: University Micro-films International, 1986], p. 1).

Preface

In what surely ranks as one of the most colossal blunders of contemporary journalism, the *International Herald Tribune* of December 27, 1991, identified Andrei Sakharov and Arseny Roginsky as leaders of "the hard line, backward-looking society called Pamyat." Not until January 7, 1992, in a little-noticed "correction" did the paper endeavor to set things straight, albeit imperfectly. The fact is that Sakharov and Roginsky were spiritual and intellectual leaders of "Memorial, a progressive group active in Russia," the very nemesis of "the reactionary group Pamyat." If it is that easy for one of the world's premier newspapers to confuse the monstrously racist group Pamyat with the human rights organization Memorial, the world cannot be blamed for its ignorance about the struggle against state terrorism in the former Soviet Union that the All-Union Society Memorial has been waging. To inform the world of Memorial's struggle for justice and reconstruction, I have written this book.

Memorial was born of the tears of those who suffered the terror of Soviet labor camps, prisons, and asylums under Stalin and his only slightly less blood-thirsty successors. Memorial (the word means the same in Russian and English) began modestly as a citizens' initiative in 1987. Initially it was little more than a campaign to collect signatures and funds for the erection of a monument honoring the victims of Soviet state terror. Memorial accomplished that in 1990. The vacant pedestal on which once stood the statue of Felix Dzerzhinsky, founder of the infamous KGB, still faces KGB headquarters. Beside it has been erected the long-embattled Memorial monument, facing the world. But Memorial has accomplished much more. Like the tiny acorn that during its growth splits the mighty granite, it has laid bare the murderous legacy of Bolshevism and is providing succor for its victims.

Memorial is an important part of Soviet history, of world history. Preceding the collapse of the Berlin Wall by two years, and as an inevitable outgrowth of glasnost, Memorial unlocked the dark secrets of a sinister past. Yet it also criticized the present and, with its modest monument on Dzerzhinsky Square, laid the cornerstone for the future. Here is the story of Memorial.

Acknowledgments

To the extent that this undertaking is true to its purpose, it captures the authentic voices of some extraordinary people. To that end they stand as co-authors of this book. Although they are quoted by name in the text, they deserve special acknowledgment here: Alexander Vologodsky, Darya Khubova, Alexander Krushelnitsky, Nikita Okhotin, Nikita Petrov, and Arseny Roginsky. Semyon Gluzman, who prevailed over the terror to become an informed healer, helped me to see things with a special vision. From my undergraduate classes at Barnard College, Columbia University, through graduate school and beyond, Jonathan Sanders has provided inspired teaching, guidance, and friendship from Manhattan to Moscow. Marc Jansen's critical challenges helped me greatly in completing my task; Robert van Voren gave me initial encouragement; my editor, Anne Kiefer, provided confidence and enthusiasm; Julie Cullen smoothly guided the book through production. Robert Knijff, my husband, documented my research in the Soviet Union with his camera and an acute observer's eye, and my family gave what families give best—unconditional support. Finally—and with no sense of finality—this book recognizes the numberless victims of terror, anytime, anywhere. We will never know all their names, but this historical chronicle recounts their story.

VICTIMS OF
SOVIET TERROR

Introduction

On August 12, 1981, Arseny Borisovich Roginsky was arrested in Leningrad on charges he had violated Article 196 of the Soviet Criminal Code—"forgery and the production and sale of forged documents."[1] But the documents to which this referred were not subversive in any conventional sense. Rather, they were letters needed to obtain permission to use the Leningrad archives for research. As a young historian Roginsky was trying to collect information about his father, who had been incriminated as an "enemy of the people," sentenced to a labor camp, and subsequently executed. Roginsky's previous efforts to research his father's history had aroused the suspicion of the Leningrad KGB, which blocked his acceptance to Leningrad University. Nevertheless, Roginsky successfully graduated from Tartu University.

While Roginsky was pursuing his studies, his research into the history of early 19th century Russia was recognized as promising by his university supervisors as well as the foreign scholars with whom he met. It was suggested that he work in the Leningrad archive after graduation, but he had two impediments. As a Jew and as the son of a former political prisoner, he was barred from work in any Soviet research institutions.[2] Roginsky's impassioned final speech at his trial did not focus on the concrete details of his case. The particulars had already been prejudged. He had been regularly harassed since 1977 with apartment searches. During a 1979 search the KGB had confiscated some books and Roginsky subsequently lost his job as a teacher. In 1981 he was presented the choice of emigration or arrest—a familiar ultimatum. Roginsky did not dwell on the exaggerated charges. He focused instead on the underlying moral principles, the very principles on which the later Memorial would be based.

Roginsky's speech, written while he was imprisoned in an eight-square-meter cell that held nine people, concentrated on the issue of gaining access to archives in the Soviet Union. He argued that archives were a natural extension of libraries, stressing that "all documents are important, all documents are valuable as witness to our past." Roginsky described the Kafkaesque rules of access to libraries—that one had to already belong to a research institution and have an "assignment" from that organization pertinent to the materials in the archive. Hence, for a historian not employed in a "scholarly institution," access was barred. Regarding the use of Soviet libraries, absurdity becomes the norm, as illustrated by the example of an American scholar working in the Soviet Union who could not get permission to read his own book![3]

Despite an eloquently presented argument on the right to study archives and to freely publish their contents so that the truth about the past might be known, Arseny Roginsky was sentenced on December 5, 1981, to four years of labor camp.[4] Ten years later, he would become one of a select few researchers to gain access to examine the KGB archives on the Stalinist past. But let us not get ahead of ourselves. To understand this story, we need to begin at another place.

Every history is a narrative journey that starts out at a specified time from a particular place. Although life is lived forward, history is written retrospectively; thus, the question about where to locate the beginning of an event is always based on the perspective and interests of the present. When did the Great Terror begin? In 1937—at the height of the purges? For Evgeniya Ginzburg, a communist and intellectual who spent eighteen years in Siberian labor camps, "the year 1937 really began on the 1st of December 1934."[5] That was the day she heard that Sergei Kirov, first secretary of the Leningrad Party, had been murdered. This marked the beginning of a new phase of terror and repression from above—one that would claim the lives of what is estimated to be over 20 million innocent people. But it has been argued that 1937 started long before 1934 and continued long after 1953 (the year of Stalin's death).

This is one of the fundamental questions with which the All-Union (now Interrepublic) voluntary historical enlightenment society known as Memorial struggles. Memorial began in August 1987 as an initiative group of eleven persons who conducted a campaign aimed at gathering signatures to support the creation of a monument to the victims of Stalin's repressions.

Arseny Roginsky, secretary of the historical committee of Memorial, explains that in the beginning people became united around the idea of the necessity for such a monument.[6] The monument would be related to the Stalinist Terror as concrete action is to thought, as ritual is to belief, a physical expression of an ineffable idea. Then, gradually, after much discussion the sentiment shifted toward creating a memorial complex similar to Yad Vashem, the Israeli monument to victims of the holocaust. This would be a public, scientific research center in Moscow that would encompass an open archive, museum, and library with information and data on victims of Stalinism.

In this regard, a historical and practical question is how one defines Stalinism. Roginsky points out that for some Stalinism is simply the personal evil of Stalin; but for others it is a much larger phenomenon. For some the repression started in 1935 or, at the earliest, 1930 with collectivization, while for others it started with the "Red Terror" in the early days of the Soviet state. For some it ended with Stalin's death, while for others its consequences still persist. "As a result," Roginsky explains, "we understand the term Stalinism in its larger context in accordance with A. D. Sakharov's definition of 'illegal and terroristic methods of governing'."[7] He makes the distinction between the victims of the repression of Stalin (the person) and the victims of Stalinism (the system). (We need only remember his own fate.) Memorial focuses on the latter, broader concept.

After the 19th Party Conference in 1988, when Gorbachev endorsed the general idea of such a memorial complex, the group gained in status and popularity. Within the space of a year and a half Memorial could count 15–20,000 active supporters from all republics and it attracted such prominent figures as the historian Yuri Afanasyev, the physicist and human rights leader Andrei Sakharov, the poet Yevgeny Yevtushenko, and the politician Boris Yeltsin. They all lent their support to the goal of building a monument.

Memorial held its Founding Conference on January 28–29, 1989. At this session, Memorial adopted a charter that committed it to establishing historical truths and promoting moral principles. A chief principle was the condemnation of arbitrariness and force as a means of dealing with social problems and social conflicts. It dared to hope that historical enlightenment would lead to political change. The mandate of the charter provides a two-fold approach to Stalinism: Memorial first seeks to establish historical truths about the crimes of Stalinism; second, it aims to use this knowledge to prevent the repetition of such mistakes through the dissemination of information. Indeed, Memorial hopes to institute fundamental changes in the sociocultural structures that enabled the Stalinist system to develop and stabilize. As a historical society examining survivors and survivals of repression, it looks to the past for answers to the present. As a political movement it has itself struggled for survival. Its future is irrevocably tied to the democratization of the successor state(s) of the former Soviet Union. In this book, I will describe Memorial as a movement of historical reflection, political criticism and idealistic hope in constant dialogue with the Soviet past, present and future, respectively.

As George Santayana cautions, "Those who cannot remember the past are condemned to repeat it." A scrupulous, courageous and unflinching remembrance of things past is the process that Memorial attempts to promote. But looking at the past can seem deceptively simple. What past are we looking at, and what *really* happened? That is a political as well as an epistemological issue. In a sense, all history is revisionist in that it formulates the past in the ever-changing, emergent perspective of the present. Put differently, it can be characterized as a dialectic between the past and the present. Memorial is engaged in a continuous dialogue with the stifled screams of the Soviet past.

In order to more fully understand the raison d'être, development, vicissitudes and ramifications of Memorial, we must first establish a frame of reference. The larger scope of events of the Stalin era (1924–1953), the phenomenon of Stalinism, and the question of its possible origins in Leninism and/or Marxism will be surveyed. Khrushchev's attempt at de-Stalinization as well as the second period of de-Stalinization under Mikhail S. Gorbachev's policy of glasnost will also be reviewed.

By 1990 glasnost (openness) had enabled Memorial to emerge and gain some popular acceptance, but perestroika (re-structuring) had not yet sanctioned its legalization. In our examination of Memorial we will begin by looking at the emergence of the organization, its charter, basic moral principles and strategies. This is based on its own documents as well as a number of Soviet and Western newspaper articles from it and about it. We will then examine Memorial as a historical society, focusing on its methods of collecting information. Often it must depend on eye-witness accounts and oral history, since so much of the vital material has either been destroyed or is sequestered in inaccessible archives. A further look at Memorial's projects (museum, library, archive) as well as its international connections should provide us with a broader picture of the historical society's goals. Much of my research on Memorial is based on first-hand observation and covers the period from its inception through the dissolution of the Soviet Union.

Finally, I will examine the political nature of Memorial even though many of its members do not want it to be viewed in this way. In a late 1989 exchange with Sakharov's widow, Yelena Bonner, Gorbachev expressed his grief and described a number of ways in which Sakharov's memory would be honored. Her response was simple and eloquent: "It would be better to register Memorial."[8] This did eventually happen, but not until 1991. A chronicle of Memorial's struggle for legal status will provide some insight into the centrality of the moral concerns stirred to a political boiling point by Memorial. I shall briefly cover the issue, which some in the organization have raised, of posthumously putting Stalin and Stalinism on trial. Their aim is not primarily vengeance or even restitution; the first would be insufficient and the second impossible. Rather, it is the empowerment of the common man to ask questions of the government, to examine archives, in sum to institutionalize accountability.

At the borderline between ontology and perception is the philosophical question, "If a tree falls in a forest and no one is there to hear it, does it make a sound?" For decades there has been an eerie silence in the forests of Katyn and Kuropaty, on the banks of the River Ob, in the fields of Rutchenko, on Golden Mountain, in the interrogation cells of the Lubyanka. Memorial has been monitoring and retrieving the dying echoes of the fallen inhabitants of these decimated landscapes. The reverberating transmissions—letters, photos, personal disclosures—still haunt the air, mocking the traditional official silence. Is this quest for enlightenment historical or political? That may be a scholastic distinction without a functional difference. This concept was grasped in one of the early Soviet anti-Stalin works whose title, *Let History Judge*,[9] recognizes the truism that all history is political judgment.

NOTES

1. Another allegation involved sending these materials abroad to anti-Soviet publications such as *Pamyat* (Memory).

2. Yevgeny Beshenkovsky, Natalya Chevinskaya, Nina Perlina, letter (public appeal) of August 16, 1981.

3. Ibid.

4. The story of Roginsky is based on various appeals that were published in the West by Helsinki Watch and others. The material was provided by CBS News Moscow.

5. Evgeniya Ginzburg, *Into the Whirlwind (Krutoi Marshrut)* (London: Collins/Havill, 1967), p. 1. (In transcribing Russian names I have used the popular English spelling system except in cases where other spellings are more familiar to Western readers, i.e. "Evgeniya" instead of "Yevgeniya.")

6. Radio Liberty report of a broadcast of March 12/13, 1989, *Interview with a member of Memorial's "rabochaya kollegiya," Arseny Roginsky*, May 12, 1989.

7. Ibid.

8. Arseny Roginsky, statement made during a workshop of the Memorial work group of the Heinrich Böll Stiftung, Bonn, Germany, February 8, 1990.

9. Roy Medvedev, *Let History Judge* (New York: Alfred A. Knopf, 1971).

PART I _____

MEMORIAL: HISTORY AS
MORAL IMPERATIVE

In this section, we will traverse the seventy-year cycle from the birth
and triumph of the Bolshevik Party under Lenin to its exposure to
glasnost and disintegration under Gorbachev. In between there was
the reign of Stalin, and throughout there was the phenomenon that
came to be called Stalinism. "Terror" and "repression" were the
shaping instruments of this period. Part I will explore their form and
scope, the efforts from above to oppose them (official "de-Stalinization"), and one of the major efforts at de-Stalinization from below—
Memorial's retrospective on Soviet history. As the rulers realized all
too well, historical scholarship is always political. The hegemonic
issues are what will be selected for remembrance and how it will be
interpreted. While Memorial was exposing the past, it was also discrediting the present. Indeed, it was partly through publicizing the
perfidy of that past that the ruling clique was unseated.

CHAPTER 1 _____

The Formation of the Soviet System

In a strict sense, history is not an event but an account of an event. History is not made at the moment an event occurs; it is only made when events are conveyed to (and, more accurately, when they are registered by) a receptive audience. In other words, an event becomes history only when it is told and heard and enshrined in memory. Memorial bears that memory, invoking the power of the word to re-member a fragmented past.

The broad and detailed gyrations of Soviet history have been known and openly discussed and debated in the West since 1917. By contrast, the discussion and debate in the Soviet Union were carried on by beleaguered groups of dissidents under clandestine circumstances. Censorship—deletion and alteration—began, for the Soviets, under Lenin and continued well into the Gorbachev era. This, of course, did not prevent people from observing what was happening around them, but the ever-growing repressive apparatus made discussion of even quasi-public events risky. In consequence, ordinary conversations, especially between casual acquaintances, sometimes assumed a surrealistic quality. As one Russian put it, "It's easy to talk about the future and the present, but the past keeps changing every day."[1] Fortunately, this is becoming less circumspect since the unofficial and official versions of Soviet history are converging toward consensus. Memorial's history is the metahistory of the struggle to achieve freedom of speech. As we briefly examine the major trends characterizing the three decades of Stalin's reign, we can observe how "revolutionary violence," that is, state terror, with its Kafkaesque system of bureaucratization and denial of the truth that everyone knows, became integral parts of the Soviet system.

The period 1924–1953 in the Soviet Union was a national calamity of such evil enormity that it ranks in monstrousness with the period of Nazism in Germany. That Stalin's reign of terror was primarily fratricidal stamped it as a uniquely disastrous national tragedy. It is therefore morally and historically appropriate that the redemptive recounting of events, the telling of the true story of what happened, should come from the victims themselves. As the long-stifled conscience of a tragic period, Memorial attempts to reconstitute the wholeness of the nation by remembering what happened, how it happened and why it happened, so that it may never happen again. It is impossible to adequately summarize the magnitude of the events of the period from the beginning of the Soviet state through 1953. Instead, the discussion will be limited to the more narrow range of Stalinist hegemony that Memorial addresses and tries to redress.

Initially, the Bolshevik Party may not have been militant and self-serving in nature, but "the Civil War . . . transformed the new mass Party into a hardened and experienced machine in which loyalty to the organization came before any other consideration."[2] In early 1921, Lenin declared "revolutionary violence" essential as a means of quelling the demonstrations in Petrograd and the Kronstadt naval base revolt.[3] This strategy was illustrative of the fact that the Party was increasingly putting its own interests above those of the people it was supposed to represent. By 1921, factions within the Party were banned, and refusal to disband meant confrontation with the Secret Police, Dzerzhinsky at its head. The interrelated processes of revolutionary violence and Kafkaesque bureaucratization were established and later refined by the Bolsheviks. In an apt analysis of Franz Kafka's *Trial*, Hannah Arendt commented, "The rule of bureaucracy insured that the interpretation of the law became an instrument of lawlessness."[4] This was only the beginning.

In 1922, as Lenin lay ill, the attention of the new Soviet state began to focus on the struggle for internal succession. It is one of the ironies of history that during this time Stalin was the least prominent figure in the Politburo, while Trotsky, Zinoviev, Kamenev, Rykov and particularly Bukharin enjoyed broad popularity among the Party masses. Lenin's testament of December 25, 1922, detailed thoughtful portraits of the six contenders. Regarding Stalin, Lenin presciently stated that he was not sure that Stalin would "always be capable of using that authority with sufficient caution."[5] He did not want to see Stalin as general secretary because he was too "rude and this defect . . . becomes intolerable in a General Secretary."[6] Lenin's criticism of Stalin has long been well known in the West but suppressed in the Soviet Union. Finally, in the recent period of de-Stalinization in the Soviet Union, we can find this excerpt in a Soviet history textbook for the tenth grade:

Lenin saw the dangers in Stalin's character—rudeness, revenge and lack of culture determined more and more when he finally came to power. Those who chose Stalin as General Secretary without listening to Lenin's advice did not know then that the majority of them would later be destroyed by this man who drenched the country in blood and replaced the enlightened ideals of socialism with army barracks.[7]

The ailing Lenin saw the coming party split arising from the enmity between Stalin and Trotsky. Robert Conquest contends that the personal roots of the Great Purge extend back to this period of Stalin's bitter rivalry with Trotsky, on whom "Stalin was to concentrate, over the years, the whole power of his immense capacity for political malice."[8] In the 1930s, as the mass repression got under way, Lenin's testament was considered a fabrication, and possession of the Bulletin of the XV Congress (of 1927) in which it was copied made one subject to arrest and repression.[9]

Important to an understanding of subsequent events was Stalin's role in the succession. The precedents for the ruthless exercise of self-serving political power would set or at least refine the modus operandi for the Bolshevik Party. Trotsky and other members of the Left had opposed Lenin on issues such as the New Economic Policy (NEP), which they considered too great a concession to capitalism. The Left (Pyatakov, Krestinsky, Rakovsky, Preobrazhensky and Radek) wanted to institute, among other things, early suppression of the independent peasantry.[10] Preobrazhensky, a leading theorist, thought that the state should use its position to pump resources out of the private sector in order to finance the expanding industrial sector.[11] He also believed that industry could be created by "squeezing the funds out of the peasantry."[12] Alternatively, Bukharin, the Party's chief theorist, argued that the Party's stability depended on lasting rapprochement with the peasantry.

Initially, Zinoviev and Kamenev, Stalin's allies at the time, led most of the attacks on Trotsky, permitting Stalin to appear to be the voice of moderation.[13] Stalin seemed to oppose Zinoviev and Kamenev's request to expel Trotsky from the Party, but in the meantime he dispersed Trotsky's leading supporters on diplomatic missions abroad, leaving Trotsky vulnerable at home. By 1925 Trotsky's views were officially condemned.[14]

In 1924–1925 the Zinoviev-Kamenev-Stalin triumvirate ended. Stalin turned on his two former allies and Bukharin was thrust into co-leadership of the majority with Stalin. Bukharin, already the principal author of policies, was raised to the rank of chief theorist and received Stalin's endorsement for his economic platform of 1924–1925.[15] In numerous speeches, Bukharin explained that nothing was more harmful than failing to understand that industry was dependent on the peasant market. He understood well the problems of peasants who were afraid to accumulate goods for fear of being accused of being kulaks. Bukharin tried to allay this fear and even urged them to prosper, using the controversial words, "get rich."[16] Though Stalin supported Bukharin's agricultural policy, he disassociated himself from such extremes. At the XIV Party Congress, Bukharin was forced to withdraw these words and admit that the kulaks were "an evil to be limited and squeezed."[17] The condemnation of Bukharin at that point was specific and did not extend to his basic economic policies.[18] Moreover, at the same congress Stalin stated, "We stand, and we shall stand, for Bukharin."[19] It soon became apparent that this alliance, like all of Stalin's other alliances, was only for a duration that suited him.

Meanwhile, Zinoviev and Kamenev were forced to turn to Trotsky for support and together they formed the United Opposition. Regarding this alliance, Robert Conquest asserts that Trotsky's final mistake was to form a bloc with these two who had little credit and little to offer.[20] Conquest maintains that Zinoviev and Kamenev were only slightly less important than Trotsky as targets of the Great Purge (p. 29). In October 1926 Zinoviev, Kamenev, Trotsky, Pyatakov and others, having already been expelled from the Politburo, denounced their own offenses. In 1927 Trotsky and Zinoviev tried in vain to appeal to the "Party masses" and workers, but they were already alienated (p. 31). On November 14 of that year Zinoviev and Kamenev, along with their followers, were expelled from the Party. Trotsky departed for Alma-Ata, Zinoviev and Kamenev to the Urals, and the others to the Siberian and Asian periphery. In 1928 when Trotsky refused to stop his political activities, the Politburo expelled him from the Soviet Union, despite the efforts of Bukharin, Tomsky, Rykov and others. On January 22, 1929, Trotsky was arrested and expelled to Turkey. Stalin's violent mechanisms for dealing with opposition were not yet fully developed.

The group that enjoyed Stalin's favor at this time were those administrators willing to follow orders. Among them were men like Molotov, "Russia's best bureaucrat" (p. 32); Voroshilov, full Politburo member in 1926; Rudzutak, who took over Zinoviev's membership; Ordzhonikidze, long a member of the Central Committee; Kirov, appointed head of the Leningrad Party; Kaganovich and Mikoyan. As for Ordzhonikidze, a Georgian, Lenin had wanted to expel him from the Party in 1922 for his brutality toward Georgian communists (p. 33). This trait was probably considered an asset by Stalin. Kirov enforced Stalin's collectivization and industrialization policies, but he was not as ruthless as Stalin's other associates (p. 33). Stalin is reported to have told Yagoda that he preferred people to support him out of fear rather than conviction because the latter could change (p. 34). Fear was apparently something Stalin thought he could hold constant.

Conquest terms Lazar Kaganovich the truest Stalinist; "a clear mind and a powerful will went with a total lack of the restraints of humanity" (pp. 34–35). He undertook Stalin's most important assignments (he was first secretary of the Ukraine, 1925–1928). Kaganovich and others dissuaded Stalin from any policy of relaxation. Zhdanov displayed intelligence and fanaticism. He, along with Malenkov, Beria and Khrushchev, combined political sagacity with ruthlessness, which assured their rise to high positions in the State (p. 35). They were to play "particularly murderous" roles in the Purge (p. 35). Stalin's support group was thus chosen for their lack of scruples and their total devotion to him. They were, in effect, "a personal group of hatchet-men" (p. 36). Yezhov, whom Conquest calls a "bloodthirsty dwarf," joined the Central Committee in 1927 (p. 36). Vyshinsky, aptly termed "a rat in human form" (p. 38) was a Menshevik until the Bolshevik victory was fully established in 1921, at which time he joined the Party (p. 37). The system was selectively rewarding those with an ability and will to employ terror.

The unraveling of the Bukharin-Stalin relationship was past and pro-logue for Stalin's developing style. In 1927–1928, an acute grain shortage led to the confiscation of grain. Bukharin called for more ambitious industrial development as well as partial voluntary collectivization. The year 1928 was a pivotal one that set the tone for the Bukharin-Stalin relationship. Until this point, Stalin's policies on industry, agriculture and planning were those of Bukharin—pro-NEP, moderate, evolutionary.[21] In the winter of 1928–1929, grain collection was going badly and the question of coercive measures arose. Bukharin, Rykov and Tomsky sup-ported the original decisions of taking "extraordinary measures" because they saw the short-term necessity, but they criticized the excesses of Stalin's implementation—the victimization of middle peasants, the draco-nian coercion and disruption of markets.[22] The three objected to the continuation of grain confiscations, adding that the bureaucratization of the Party had grown and that a personal regime was being established inside the Party.[23] They resigned and refused to return to their positions. Stephen Cohen concludes that already in mid-1928, Bukharin perceived in Stalin's warfare policies "the prospect of a third revolution," civil war in the countryside, bloody suppression and a "police state. . . . This prescience alone . . . was also to earn him Stalin's special animus."[24]

Not long thereafter, the three accused, Bukharin, Rykov and Tomsky, were persuaded to submit statements admitting their mistakes. Cohen asserts that the months between April and December 1929 were among the most important in Russian history. They witnessed the radicalization of Stalin's policies, the worsening of state relations with the peasantry, the campaign against the Right opposition and Bukharin, and the demise of political moderation. This finally led to the destruction of NEP and the imposition of the revolution from above. Cohen concludes that Bukharin's defeat was a "political prelude to the 'revolution from above' and to the advent of what became known as Stalinism."[25]

Conquest explains that the XVI Party Conference of April 1929 ushered in the principles of crash industrialization and collectivization.[26] The Party had decided not to employ persuasion or economic pressure on the peasantry, but rather frontal assault—civil war in the countryside (p. 42). The skilled entrepreneur class in industry had already been destroyed by the Bolsheviks. Likewise, the most productive and efficient members of the peasantry were being eliminated. They were robbed of their incentive by Stalin's seizure of their surplus (p. 42). Collectivized farms were established by force; in retaliation, angry peasants destroyed much of Russia's agricultural wealth (p. 43). On January 5, 1930, the Central Committee decided to complete collectivization of the more important regions by the autumn of 1930 or 1931. From January to March 1930 between four and fourteen million peasant holdings were brought to collective farms. More than 50 percent of peasant households were collectivized within five months (p. 43). However, this campaign resulted in unexpected consequences. The peasants preferred to destroy their livestock, often gorging themselves rather than give it up to the state. Stalin found scapegoats for this disaster in the local Party workers on whom he put the blame for excesses. The peasants left the collectivized farms. It has been said that this would have been an opportune time for Bukharin, Rykov and Tomsky to come forward, perhaps presenting a political alternative to Stalin, but they did not (p. 44). Instead they urged patience in their followers.

Subsequently, Stalin allowed a slightly longer period for his collectivization plans, and with a "combination of ruthlessness and economic measures" he achieved almost complete collectivization of the country by

1932 (pp. 44–45). But by that time the peasants were only producing enough for subsistence, leaving nothing for the state. Thus, when local officials confiscated their sacks of grain for export, the famine was exacerbated. The 44 percent procurements of the already 12 percent below average 1932 crop created large-scale starvation. It was, as Conquest remarks, "perhaps the only case in history of a purely man-made famine" (p. 45). The Soviet government ignored the existence of the more than five million deaths from hunger and diseases of hunger, concealing it from the world (pp. 45–46).

Stalin's policies of terror compounded the plight of starvation. In August 1932 a new law imposed a ten-year sentence for any theft of grain, and deportation quotas were set. Stalin later told Churchill that ten million kulaks had to be dealt with, many were "wiped out," others were transferred to Siberia (pp. 45–46). Between 1933 and 1935 more than 3.5 million peasants were in the expanding labor camp system; 25 percent of the productive capacity of Soviet agriculture was destroyed. To hide this debacle, from 1933 on, Soviet statistics for grain output were falsified by 30 percent. Mass terror reigned in the countryside, where the police and Party officials were refining their ruthless methods of operation (p. 47).

Meanwhile, the workers were subjected to their own ordeal. In October 1930 a new decree was issued that prohibited free movement of labor. Factories were forbidden to employ people who had left their previous jobs without permission, and unemployment compensation was abolished. The year 1931 brought prison sentences for violation of labor discipline and punitive measures for negligence. Workers were held responsible for damage done to instruments and materials. Shock brigades received special rations. In 1932, three new regulations were issued to further restrict freedom: the death penalty for theft of state or collective property, instant dismissal from work for one day's unauthorized absence and the re-introduction of the internal passport system,[27] which Lenin had denounced as tsarist "backwardness and despotism."[28] This institutionalized coercion was a punitive perversion of industrial psychology.

Stalin's new style of terror had first been carried out in the countryside, but he extended his authoritarian rule to the entire industrial sector in the years before the onset of the Great Terror, despite gathering opposition. Very simply, he did this by physically destroying his enemies. There were numberless conspiracy cases of those years. The Ryutin case was an example of the terror that engulfed all the main oppositionists (pp. 51–52). A lesser Rightist group headed by Ryutin and Slepkov issued a document in 1932 proposing an economic retreat, reduction of investment in industry and the liberation of the peasants, allowing them to leave the kolkhozes. But, most important, it included a fierce condemnation of Stalin, calling for his forcible removal from the leadership. Stalin's response was swift, simple and characteristic. He called for their assassination. It is said that Kirov, Ordzhonikidze, Kuibyshev and others were against the death penalty, while Kaganovich fully supported Stalin (p. 53). The Ryutin group was expelled from the Party in October 1932 and jailed. Stalin was later to use this case to accuse the opposition of capital crimes. Indeed, in the Great Trials of 1936, 1937 and 1938 the accused routinely confessed to complicity in the Ryutin plot (p. 54).

In 1933 over 800,000 Party members were purged; in 1934, 340,000. The Smirnov "plot" was another Ryutin-type case. The Old Bolshevik was expelled from the Central Committee. It seems that even Stalin's Politburo supporters, for the most part, were not in favor of executing Bolshevik conspirators. Conquest wryly comments that "moderates" such as Kirov and others "cheerfully massacred the Whites, and at least uncomplainingly starved and slaughtered the peasantry," but horrifiedly resisted the execution of prominent Party members and "shedding the blood of Bolsheviks" (p. 57).

From 1930 on, various secret trials and executions without trial took place in the domains of economy, ideology, science, the food industry and the academic world. These served as "dress rehearsals" (p. 737) for what was to come. Some of the techniques instituted and later institutionalized included: painfully long hours of interrogation, the use of complicated, difficult-to-follow stories, the use of concentration on discrepancy in detail and the testimony of others similarly accused.

In the ensuing years, Stalin would decide that the Russian people were to blame for the country's economic woes, sparing his regime the responsibility for the debacle. Ultimately, Stalin's course was to "burn out the last roots of humanism," sparing no section of the population (p. 59). Stalin's wife, Nadezhda Alliluyeva, horrified by the sufferings of the collectivization campaign, committed suicide on November 9, 1932 (p. 104).

In 1933 there was some loosening of the repression and there were fewer peasant deportations. Kamenev and Zinoviev were brought back from Siberia, but only to confess anew. Danger of war from the rise of Nazism in Germany motivated a few oppositionists to reconcile themselves with the regime. Having won against the odds, Stalin's prestige grew (p. 62). During this period Stalin consolidated his political hold, but weakened the economy, eroded the intelligentsia, decimated the agricultural productivity and debilitated the military strength of the country.

The "unity of the Party" was celebrated at the XVII Congress of Victors in 1934. Kirov gave a speech that aroused such enthusiasm that a *Pravda* article described him as the Party's favorite (p. 65). It seemed possible in 1934 that the old Leninist cadres might solidify around Kirov to curtail Stalin's quest for unlimited authority. The challenge was countered by the dictator. The internecine struggle for control marked this "unity" congress as, in fact, a particularly characteristic example of Party disunity.

Meanwhile, from 1917 on both the size and power of the Secret Police force grew. The Cheka of 1917 was renamed the GPU (State Political Administration) in 1922. This was part of the NKVD (People's Commissariat for Internal Affairs); both were headed by Dzerzhinsky. In 1923 the GPU became the OGPU (Unified State Political Administration), which was separated from the NKVD. In theory, its function was to investigate and liquidate actions of counter-revolutionary sabotage and bring saboteurs and counter-revolutionaries to trial. In practice, it was Stalin's private enforcement cadre. Already in 1920 the police were authorized to send people to forced labor camps for up to five years by administrative decision alone if there was insufficient evidence for judicial proceedings (p. 724). By 1926 when Dzerzhinsky died, Yagoda, a chemist who would later use poison as an NKVD device (p. 724), was a rising power. Yagoda took charge of the GULAG (the Main Administration of Corrective Labor Camps). By 1933 the OGPU was given the legal right of execution and by June 1934 had established the hostage principle whereby the pressure of threats to the prisoner's relatives was employed. The following month, the OGPU was absorbed into the All-Union NKVD headed by Yagoda. He created a general police organization, a "highly paid elite" (p. 728), which administered state security. Also during this period a central Purge Commission, which included Yezhov, was established. From this came the show trial. The Shakhty engineers trial in 1928, presided over by Vyshinsky, "was the first testing ground of the more recent technique of founding a case upon false confessions extracted by terror" (p. 68).

Stalin had his apparatus of terror fully in place by the time of Kirov's assassination on December 1, 1934. It is widely believed that he hired Leonid Nikolayev to do it.

This killing has every right to be called the crime of the century. Over the next four years hundreds of Russians, including the most prominent political leaders of the Revolution, were shot for direct responsibility for the assassination and—literally—millions of others went to their deaths for complicity in one or another part of the vast conspiracy which allegedly lay behind it (p. 73).

Stalin was demonstrating with increasing proficiency how the use of mass terror could strengthen his grip on political power. Fatal car accidents and other mishaps were arranged to eliminate those who knew or were thought to know too much about the murder. Thousands of political suspects were imprisoned (p. 84). After the attempt on Lenin's life in 1918, Sverdlov, the Bolshevik leader's lieutenant, called for "merciless mass terror." There was little Bolshevik protest when hundreds of prisoners, White Guards, and the like were shot (p. 84).

The Soviet press joined in the mass accusations, calling for a ruthless battle against the hidden enemy and attacking Trotskyites. A torrent of announcements of trials of conspirators, the NKVD Leningrad leadership among others, were being published. Between thirty and forty thousand Leningraders were deported en masse to Siberia and the Arctic within the space of a few months. In early 1935 Stalin reshuffled his subordinates and tightened his grip. Yezhov was appointed to head the Party Control Commission; Kaganovich's protege, Nikita Khrushchev, was made the first secretary of the Moscow Party organization; Vyshinsky became the prosecutor general and Georgi Malenkov became Yezhov's chief deputy of the Cadres Department of the Central Committee. In March 1935 the works of Trotsky, Zinoviev and Kamenev were removed from library shelves. As of April 7, 1935, all penalties, including the death penalty, could be applied to children down to twelve years of age (p. 129). A decree in June of that year incorporated the death penalty into the Criminal Code for civil and military flight abroad; the military's families were subjected to ten years' imprisonment and civilians' families to five years' exile (p. 128). The hostage system proved an effective means for the authorities to obtain desired confessions.

There was a brief respite from repression between July 1935 and August 1936 as Stalin prepared for the Great Purge (pp. 133–134). The dictator set up mechanisms for the direct control of the Secret Police, the Party and the state hierarchy. Fake trials for political purposes were established, and the purge operators perfected the use of torture, blackmail and falsification of evidence (p. 135).

In June 1936, Stalin was still having some trouble obtaining confessions from political enemies like Kamenev. Finally, when Yezhov threatened to shoot Kamenev's son, the accused agreed to come to trial if Stalin publicly promised not to execute them or their followers. The court was packed with spectators chosen by the NKVD as well as NKVD clerks and officials. Vituperative press campaigns were conducted to prepare the public for the harshness of the sentences that had been prepared beforehand. Consequently Zinoviev, Kamenev and others confessed their roles in Kirov's assassination, plans to kill Stalin, Molotov, and others.[29] They then received the death penalty. In many cases the only evidence against the accused was their own and others' confessions.[30] Vyshinsky considered a confession in itself, no matter how obtained, to be grounds for conviction,[31] A week after Zinoviev's execution, Stalin instructed Yagoda to select and shoot 5,000 oppositionists in camps.[32] Even the Secret Police were not immune from Stalin's rule of terror. In 1936 Stalin began his attack on Yagoda, appointing Yezhov as people's commissar for internal affairs.

The question of why people confessed, often to imaginary crimes, knowing that this would mean death, is not as puzzling as it seems. In fact, the prisoners' choices were very limited. They were under the complete control of the NKVD, which had already condemned them to death. A confession meant a quick death; resistance usually meant a slower death. In some cases, prisoners felt ideologically motivated. Many of the prominent communists of the Great Trials of 1936, 1937 and 1938 had abiding faith in and loyalty to the Party and hoped that by sacrificing themselves they might preserve the Party's unity.[33] Perhaps the most plausible explanation lies in the calculated willingness of Stalin and the NKVD to exceed the psychological and physical pain threshold of their broken victims.

The basic method of obtaining confessions was the conveyor—hours and days of relentless interrogation, lack of sleep and food. The inevitable physical exhaustion eroded physical and psychological resistance.[34] In addition, the refined physical torture broke the prisoners' wills so that many felt that death would be a welcome relief from the pain, humiliation and torment. Others, not yet arrested, stayed awake for days and nights anticipating the ominous visit by the NKVD. For those prisoners who could withstand the physical torture, a psychological one was added: they were told that their families would be tortured and killed, and in some cases this happened. In using relatives as hostages, Stalin recognized no limits. To him belongs the credit for this "new development in Russian history."[35] Given the circumstances of complete and ruthless control, there was no viable alternative to confession.

By August 21, 1936, the newspapers published the order from Prosecutor Vyshinsky initiating a new investigation of the connections of Bukharin, Rykov, Tomsky and others with "despicable terrorists." Medvedev notes that "the same issue of *Izvestiya* that included this demand in its lead article listed Bukharin as editor-in-chief on the last page."[36] By January 16, 1937, *Izvestiya* appeared without Bukharin's signature. Even before he was arrested, he was proclaimed "enemy of the people." Stalin's attack on the Rightists continued to gain momentum. On January 30, Pyatakov and other Old Bolsheviks were sentenced to death. Ordzhonikidze protested and fomented opposition in Party circles. It was to no avail. As Conquest points out, it only allowed Stalin to build his case against Ordzhonikidze.[37] One afternoon, Ordzhonikidze was found dead of a "heart attack" in his home (p. 260). By the time of his arrest, Bukharin declared that a conspiracy did indeed exist, and he accused Stalin and Yezhov of being its leaders and plotting to install an NKVD regime (p. 270). Bukharin and Rykov were taken to the Lubyanka on February 27, 1937. They did not return.

In the autumn of 1936, Stalin had to attempt to justify arresting and trying potential rivals. But by early 1937 he was able to have close colleagues arrested without consulting anyone. Conquest marks the transition from despotism to "absolute autocracy" as the 1937 February–March plenum (p. 274). Thereafter, Stalin purged Yagoda's old NKVD by sending departmental chiefs on inspection assignments to various parts of the country and having them arrested at the first train stations (p. 275). Three thousand of Yagoda's NKVD officials were executed in 1937 (p. 275) and, of course, Yagoda himself was arrested. Vyshinsky had to repeatedly overhaul the prosecution apparatus, getting rid of prosecutors who still wished to maintain some semblance of legality (p. 276).

On June 11, 1937, many of the professional soldiers of the Red Army Command, including Marshall Tukhachevsky and others, those who had developed and organized a modern and efficient army, were charged with treason, tried and executed the next day (p. 277). Many of their wives and children were sent to camps. Stalin accused Tukhachevsky of colluding with the Germans in a planned coup d'état. A story was fabricated detailing the "counter-revolutionary military fascist organization in the armed forces" (p. 293).

Some have suggested that Stalin purged the army in order to give himself the freedom to consummate the Nazi-Soviet Pact of 1939 (p. 297). Based on the categories of arrestees (i.e., foreign communists), prisoners were predicting the pact in 1938 (p. 298). Paradoxically, a new popular charge of "Nazi connections" was substituted for "Trotskyite terrorism" (p. 305). It was clear from Tukhachevsky's arrest that the NKVD had won control (p. 315). Even as the generals were being executed, Stalin and Yezhov launched an NKVD campaign against the officer corps (p. 310). All military intelligence agents abroad were recalled and shot. V. A. Antonov-Ovseenko, the Soviet consul-general in Spain, perished at this time as well. He was held in the Butyrka but refused to sign anything. The protocols of his interrogation were 300 pages (p. 611). His foster daughter has become an active member of Memorial, sharing her experience of his plight with both new and newly receptive audiences. An equally sweeping purge of the navy took place. No admirals survived. While others fell, Khrushchev and Brezhnev survived and rose in power.

Roy Medvedev asserts that lists containing 40,000 names went to Stalin for approval for execution (p. 354). Fear pervaded the country at all levels. For every Party member who suffered, eight to ten ordinary citizens were imprisoned (p. 375). The Stalinist totalitarianism promoted the worst traits of the worst people by providing an outlet for the sadist and encouraging the mean and malicious (pp. 378–379). Stalin required not only submission but complicity. All those arrested had to denounce others, and every denunciation resulted in more arrests. Automatic suspects included: active members of the church, members of religious sects, rebels (i.e., anyone who in the past had in any way been involved in an anti-Soviet uprising), those who had contacts abroad, all former members of noncommunist parties, active members of student corporations, the National Guard, anyone who had fought against the Reds in the Civil War, representatives of foreign firms, anyone who had contact with foreign countries (i.e., businessmen, hotel/restaurant owners, shopkeepers, bankers, clergy, the former Red Cross). In total, this amounted to 23 percent of the population plus their acquaintances (pp. 385–386)! When people in the Baltic states were arrested they were immediately deported to a camp and their families were sent to a special settlement. By the autumn of 1937 writers and journalists were disappearing. Name plates could not be put on the office doors of departmental heads at *Izvestiya* until 1939 (p. 386).

The arrest procedure was starkly routine. Normally, two or three NKVD men would knock on the door, enter someone's home, then search through books and documents while keeping the victim and his wife under guard. Then they would leave with the victim without telling his family where he was being taken. The families had to go from prison to prison trying to get information. There they would stand in lines to give the fifty rubles per month to which prisoners were entitled. Among this group was Anna Akhmatova, whose son, Gumilyov, was in jail in 1940. She requested that if a monument to her was ever put up, it should stand in front of the prison gates in Leningrad where she stood for three hundred hours (p. 392). Rumors of the existence of certain camps, gathered from other wives, were sometimes the only source of information for tracing husbands.

What were the prisons themselves like? Initially, the prisoner signed in and was searched. Cells were also searched regularly. The cells were intensely overcrowded; Tsarist prison conditions have been described as better (p. 393). In Moscow, for example, a cell meant for 24 held at least 140 by November 1937; a women's cell for 25 held 110. There were few beds, and prisoners had to sleep on their sides for lack of space. It was even worse in Leningrad, Kharkov and provincial jails. A Kharkov prison for 800 held 12,000 by 1937 (p. 394). The food rations were minimal but supposedly good in comparison with the camps where the "diet seems to have been calculated to be just enough to keep a more or less motionless prisoner alive" (p. 395). Disease, of course, was rampant. Through it all, there seems to have been some sort of prison camaraderie—lectures were given, stories told, and forbidden games were played clandestinely. Books were available in the Lubyanka and the Butyrka, though this was stopped at the height of Yezhov's power. He also had all the windows blocked with shutters. After the Bukharin trial, these shutters were open for only ten minutes a day (p. 397). The slightest offense could send the prisoner to the punishment cells where the meager food ration was decreased by one-half to two-thirds, outer clothing was removed, and the prisoner could only lie down at night on the stone floor (p. 397). There were also inner prisons— that is, prisons within prisons, which inmates termed "living graves." Here no noise was permitted, one could sit during the day but not lean, and total isolation was imposed upon the prisoner.

Of the three main Moscow prisons, Lefortovo was apparently the great torture center. The Lubyanka was similar but on a lesser scale and the Butyrka had a special section for "politicals" only. This category included anyone potentially capable of opposing the system. Some prisoners who had performed unsatisfactorily in the preliminary investigation at Lubyanka were transferred to Lefortovo (p. 400). The Shpalerny prison was Leningrad's equivalent to the Lubyanka, the Kresti to the Butyrka. The one-man cells of Tsarist times housed sixteen during this period (pp. 401–402). Transfer prisons held those sentenced to camps.

A measure of the total Kafkaesque madness of these years is evident in the fact that sometimes the inmate only discovered what his crimes might be through discussions with cellmates, and as Conquest asserts, "the chances of anyone there being actually guilty of anything whatever were very small" (p. 402). Even a veterinarian who had treated consular dogs or a woman who supplied the German consul's milk, or her brother(!), were subject to arrest. Greeks, Chinese, Armenians, Latvians, national minorities, Jews, Jehovah's witnesses, Buddhists (as Japanese agents), engineers, and anyone connected with production were all arrested. Eight years was a usual sentence for the wife of an "enemy of the people" (p. 407). In 1939 when reports of the arrests of NKVD officers for extorting false confessions reached the public, so too did related stories of mass trials of children surface: 160 children between the ages of twelve and fourteen were arrested and severely interrogated (p. 409). After this they confessed to espionage, terror, treason, links with the Gestapo, and the like (p. 409).

Accidents that occurred every five minutes somewhere on the Russian railway system led to the slaughter of railway cadres, because Kaganovich asserted that every railway system shows "Trotskyite-Japanese sabotage" (p. 411).

In order to deflect criticism, the Purge was largely blamed on Yezhov, the head of the NKVD, and his campaign of repression came to be known as Yezhovshchina. The public relations ruse was partially successful in that many people actually believed that Stalin did not know. Stalin was able to maintain this myth by purging the Secret Police in 1938 and having history books rewritten to portray himself as a hero of the revolution.

The legitimacy of the NKVD interrogations was supported by Vyshinsky's assertion that a confession was sufficient grounds for incrimination and could serve to implicate others. The accused was not told why he was there; he had to build his own case against himself. The questions drew on an ancient if dishonorable heritage based on questionnaires used in the Holy Inquisition (p. 414). Many of the early NKVD officers who knew of the deception were themselves purged. Later Stalinists believed in, or at least convinced themselves of, the accused's guilt. By August 1937, when arrests had outpaced the interrogative capacity of the NKVD, beating was employed to extract confessions. It appears that at the beginning of that year Stalin issued instructions to use torture (p. 416). The few humane officers and guards did not survive Yezhov's purge of the NKVD. The triumvirate of Bolshevik policy—revolutionary violence, bureaucratization, and ruthlessness—achieved full and corrupt power.

By the time of Yezhov's fall, no less than 5 percent of the population were on NKVD lists. Those who had formerly been listed as Trotskyites were reallocated to some other category because the Trotskyite quota had been exceeded. Death penalties were estimated as not more than 10 percent, though in Gorky at the height of the Purge fifty to seventy corpses were removed daily from NKVD headquarters (p. 427).

The Purge reached down into the mass of peasantry and ordinary workers. But the hardest hit was the urban population, particularly the educated classes and members of the intelligentsia such as historians and writers (p. 430). Writers (and particularly historians, as chroniclers of events) have always been the culpable messengers in the Soviet state. The intellectual section of the apparatus was replaced with Stalin's "creatures" (p. 436). Out of seven hundred writers at the First Writers Congress of 1934, only fifty saw the second in 1954 (p. 437).

Writers such as Babel, Zamyatin and Osip Mandelshtam were under attack. Pasternak refused to sign a list of those who applauded the execution of the generals, but it seems that the organizers added his name anyway (p. 447). Gorky, a favorite of Stalin, is said to have intervened to help his colleagues. Conductors, actors, ballerinas and their husbands and wives were repressed, many for their contact with foreigners. Robert Conquest, the chief source of material for this section, poignantly states that "the few we have spoken of, and briefly, must stand for a holocaust of the things of the spirit" (p. 449). They were not the tip of the iceberg, rather the top of the pyre. Indeed, Stalin was the master of the Pyrrhic victory.

Once the prisoners had confessed, if they escaped execution they were sent off to corrective labor camps in the north. The vast empty spaces of the Urals, Arkhangelsk, and the gold fields of Kolyma came under NKVD control. These northern camps were separated from the rest of the country by great stretches of no-man's-land inhabited only by cannibal tribes and the like (p. 473). The camps were of three types: factory and agricultural colonies, camps for mass work (in distant regions for "class dangerous elements") and punitive camps of strict isolation for those who had already been through the other colonies. One wonders how so many in the West could have been so ill-informed about this vast system that repressed millions of people. Yet they were, despite the fact that the labor camp was both an economic and political pillar of Stalin's regime. Through some combination of Stalin's careful concealment (p. 450) and the West's careless scrutiny, the system remained a well-kept secret to outsiders.

In the first half of the 1930s, the camps were mostly filled with the peasantry. The first death camp—Kholmogory, near Arkhangelsk—was already in operation in 1921. Additionally, the Gulag administered sixty-five concentration camps in 1922, all under the NKVD. The first great camps were the Solovetsky monasteries in the far north. Average life expectancy in the camps between 1929 and 1934 was one to two years (p. 454). Conquest presents the following statistics on the average number of prisoners in labor camps and places of detention: 1928, 30,000; 1930, 600,000; 1931–1932, two million; 1933–1935, five million; 1935–1937, six million. He contrasts these figures with the maximum number of forced labor prisoners—32,000 in 1912—and the maximum total of 183,949 prisoners in Tsarist times (p. 454).

The journey itself to the camps produced a high death rate. It could take months of being crammed into a railroad car with inadequate food, water and sanitation. Within the camps themselves, the 10–15 percent real criminal element ruled the rest of the prison population—murdering, robbing and beating other prisoners. The politicals were given the heavy work, and the criminals received the lighter load (p. 458).

Life in the camps was both difficult and dangerous. Refusal to work could lead to immediate execution or solitary confinement. A second offense meant death. There was a quota for the number of people allowed to be out sick—one had to be dying to be allowed to go to the infirmary, and not even that guaranteed entrance (p. 466). Prisoners were given rewards of food for turning in escaped fellow prisoners. In addition, the NKVD charged guards with complicity in any prisoner's escape.

In camps like Kolyma, 8 to 9 days from Vladivostok by boat—what A. D. Sakharov called the death ship (p. 475)—where temperatures went down to as low as –70 degrees Celsius, the death rate was 30 percent per annum. The meager food ration, just above starvation level, was only given if the prisoners had fulfilled the norm during their twelve- to sixteen-hour work day. In addition, in the lumber camps, the concept of collective responsibility for work was invoked. The inadequate work of one individual could mean that all starved.

These millions of slave laborers, a large proportion of whom built the Kotlas-Vorkuta railway, became an essential component of the Soviet economy during these years. The life expectancy on this particular railway was three months. Stalin knew that Marx objected to slavery, because its lack of incentives led to inefficiency, so he linked prisoners' food rations to output (p. 483). Conquest provides the following statistics on excess deaths due to forced labor camps and settlements: 1927–1938, 2.3 million; 1936–1939, 2.8 million; 1939–1941, 1.8 million (p. 493). He concludes that three million died by execution or attrition in camps in the two-year Yezhov period (p. 495).

The Purge continued to operate both at home and abroad, extending to the Comintern for their contact with foreigners. Even many Jews were arrested on charges of fascist espionage (p. 578). After the 1939 Nazi-Soviet Pact the NKVD provided lists to the Gestapo, and many German communists were betrayed to the Nazis. The heaviest casualties of foreign communists in the Soviet Union befell the Poles (p. 582). Yezhov also organized mobile groups charged with assassination outside Russia. In their turn, NKVD men abroad were sometimes recalled to Moscow and executed. But one of Stalin's main problems abroad was that Trotsky was still alive. The Trotsky dossier alone occupied three floors of the NKVD at No. 2 Dzerzhinsky (p. 599). On February 14, 1938, Trotsky's son died under mysterious circumstances in a Paris hospital (p. 598). A large operation was devoted to the elimination of Trotsky. It was eventually successful in Mexico in August 1940.

Beria's appointment on July 20, 1938, marked the beginning of Yezhov's decline. There was a rumor that Yezhov and Kaganovich had clashed on the issue of power and that even Stalin found the extent of Yezhov's purge too vast (pp. 607–609). On December 8, 1938, it was announced that "the rule, at once pettifogging and bloodthirsty, of the horrible Yezhov had come to an end" (p. 622). Beria's appointment marked the end of the Great Purge. Some NKVD interrogators were shot for extracting false confessions by violence. Although there were a smaller number of arrests in towns and villages thereafter, that was still enough to maintain a pervasive atmosphere of submission and silence (p. 627). By the XVIII Party Congress of March 10–21, 1939, Stalin had completed his consolidation of power (1,108 of the 1,966 delegates from the previous congress had been arrested). Khrushchev asserted that 98 percent of the 1934 Central Committee had been shot (p. 632). In 1939 Khrushchev and Zhdanov attained full membership in the Politburo. That same year, on August 23, the Soviets and Germans signed the fateful Molotov-Ribbentrop pact, dividing Europe into Soviet and Nazi spheres of influence. The following year, the German intelligence service estimated that it would take four years before the Soviet Army returned to its 1937 level of efficiency. Meanwhile, a million prisoners a year were still being dispatched to replace those who had died (p. 641). The period 1939–1941 brought mass deportations of Poles, Balts and other minorities. Stalin, during this time, refused to believe Soviet and Western intelligence reports that the Nazis were preparing to attack Russia. Hitler was apparently a man Stalin felt he could trust.

World War II broke upon the Russians at a time when the people had not yet recovered from Stalin's purges, and the government was viewed not as a source of help but as a source of threat. Consequently, the war mobilization was considered by many as a kind of liberation; religion was reinstated and images of Mother Russia helped to support the war effort. Stalin capitalized on the outside threat by glorifying himself, building his cult of personality.

However, despite an external enemy, Stalin continued his internal repression. In 1943–1944, the populations of seven entire nations (mainly from the Caucasus) were arrested and deported (p. 645). When, in 1943, the Germans announced the discovery of mass graves containing the remains of at least 5,000 (out of a probable 15,000) executed Polish officers and soldiers in the Katyn forest near Smolensk, the Russians responded that they had been left behind in the camps and fell into German hands (p. 642). At the time, this was accepted by the Western press and Allies who felt that unity against Hitler was essential. Though the fact has long been known in the West that these were victims of the NKVD, shot in April or May 1940, it was not acknowledged by the Soviet Union until 1990.[38]

The postwar years brought further repression as a wave of arrests in 1946–1947 struck Jews, army officers and others. Few of the prisoners sentenced to camps in 1945–1946 survived until 1953.[39] In 1947 famine struck, decreasing already minimal camp rations. The beginning of the 1950s saw a small drop in the camp death rate, but there were almost no releases; this resulted in a maximum camp population by 1953, the year of Stalin's death. In the new society created by Stalin, forced labor had become a permanent economic structure.[40] Stalin had established both a command economy and the subordination of all levels of society to the political machine. But the economic advantages of this were nil. Whatever basic economic benefits were achieved during the Stalinist regime were already in place before the Purge proper started. In 1952–1953, hundreds died as Jewish intellectuals were targeted in the Doctors Plot. The instruction to the NKVD, Khrushchev later revealed, was "Beat, beat and beat again."[41] In 1952, the chief Yiddish writers were executed in the "Crimean Affair" for not betraying their language and literature.[42]

Stalin died on March 5, 1953, ending the dictatorship under which immeasurable loss of humanity and humankind occurred. How many indeed did fall victim to the cruelty of this period? Robert Conquest estimates a total of over 20 million victims, including those lost by collectivization and famine.[43] In the Soviet Union a number of sources, including the surviving victims themselves or their families, have become available in recent years to aid in research. They have furnished astonishing statistics. Various figures have been cited. They range from 3 million to 60 million (averaging about 20 million) victims of Stalinist repression between the years 1918 and 1956 (see Appendix A).

Alec Nove's words provide a raison d'être for Memorial: "an honest examination of the past, in all its complexity, is seen as a precondition for necessary societal change; it is a sort of exorcism."[44] Unfortunately, by the time exorcism was considered a possibility, as these depredations attest, the body as well as the soul of Russia had been ravaged beyond the healing power attendant to the simple removal of the evil spirit. Where Louis XIV's boast that "L'Etat c'est moi" (I am the state) was vainglorious, Stalin had triumphed in this incarnation. Whether we are discussing a few million or tens of millions of victims, by the time of Stalin's death in 1953 the Soviet political organization had been transmogrified into the evil spirit of Josef Stalin and the machine of centralized, one-party, all-pervasive rule which he created continued to govern the country. More than exorcism would be needed. It would require a post-mortem dissection of the morbid anatomy. Memorial is the pathologist.

NOTES

1. *International Herald Tribune*, 27 July 1990.

2. Robert Conquest, *The Great Terror* (Middlesex, England: Penguin Books, 1968), p. 22.

3. Ibid., pp. 23–24.

4. Hannah Arendt, "Franz Kafka," in *Franz Kafka: An Anthology of Marxist Criticism*, ed. Kenneth Hughes (Hanover and London: University Press of New England, 1981), pp. 4–5.

5. Moshe Lewin, *Lenin's Last Struggle* (New York and London: Monthly Review Press, 1968), p. 80.

6. Ibid., p. 84.

7. Y. S. Borisov, *Istoriya SSSR: materialy k uchebniku dlya devyatogo klassa sredney shkoly* (Moscow: Prosveshcheniye, 1988), p. 275.

8. Conquest, p. 25.

9. Roy Medvedev, *Let History Judge* (New York: Alfred A. Knopf, 1971), p. 29.

10. Conquest, p. 26.

11. Stephen F. Cohen, *Bukharin and the Bolshevik Revolution* (Oxford: Oxford University Press, 1980), p. 163.

12. Conquest, p. 27.

13. Ibid., p. 28.

14. Ibid., p. 29.

15. Medvedev, p. 44.

16. Nikolai Bukharin, *Izbranniye Proizvedeniya* (Moscow: Politizdat, 1988), p. 464.

17. Alec Nove, *An Economic History of the USSR* (Middlesex, England: Penguin Books, 1969), p. 123.

18. Medvedev, p. 64.

19. Cohen, p. 215.

20. Conquest, p. 31.

21. Stephen F. Cohen, "Bolshevism and Stalinism," in *Stalinism: Essays in Historical Interpretation*, ed. Robert C. Tucker (New York: W. W. Norton & Company, 1977), pp. 21–22.

22. Cohen, *Bukharin*, p. 279.

23. Ibid., p. 305.

24. Ibid., p. 322.

25. Ibid., p. 312–313.

26. Conquest, p. 41.

27. Though internal passports became increasingly irrelevant, the system remained intact until 1992 when the Russian Constitutional Court declared it unconstitutional (*New York Times*, 27 December 1992).

28. Conquest, p. 49.

29. Medvedev, p. 168.

30. Conquest, p. 178.

31. Ibid., p. 210.

32. Ibid., p. 176.

33. Ibid., p. 189.

34. Ibid., p. 199.

35. Ibid., p. 203.

36. Medvedev, p. 170.

37. Conquest, p. 259.

38. *International Herald Tribune*, 26 March 1990.

39. Conquest, p. 658.

40. Ibid.

41. Ibid., p. 663.

42. Ibid., p. 664.

43. Robert Conquest, "The Great Terror Revised," *Survey* 16, no. 1 (Winter 1971): 94.

44. Alec Nove, *Glasnost in Action* (Boston: Unwin Hyman, 1989), p. 30.

CHAPTER 2 _____

Stalinism: Inheritance and Legacy

In the aftermath of a natural catastrophe men characteristically raise metaphysical questions, seeking to account for God's way with man. The Great Terror, a catastrophe of the magnitude of the bubonic plague, was a wholly man-made catastrophe. Inevitably it raises political questions concerning both the relationship between the individual and the collective and the relative influence of leaders and cultural movements on the course of history. What made the Great Terror so diabolical was not simply that it was engineered by a cruel despot but that it was executed by an efficient bureaucracy. The merging of ruthless coercion with routine bureaucracy is the framework through which this period of Soviet history will be explored. Differentiating Stalin from Stalinism is a difficult but useful approach.

Was the suffering inflicted on the Soviet people mainly a result of the particular personality of Josef Stalin, or was he himself swept on by a more powerful movement of forces? Was Stalinism inevitable, or at least normative, given the nature of Bolshevism or even Marxism? Or, given the lofty idealism of the founding revolutionaries, did Stalin constitute a complete abrogation of communism? In the words of Seweryn Bialer, "did Stalin create an 'ism'?," was he the "passive agent of inexorable tendencies unleashed by the October Revolution of 1917 or the creator of a separate tradition?"[1] Many historians contend that Stalinism cannot be understood as a whole; rather, its various aspects must be approached separately. This chapter will present some of the theories on the origins and nature of Stalinism. While these approaches seek to trace the roots of Stalinism,

Memorial has an additional goal. It documents and confronts the persistence of Stalinism long after the dictator's death. Whatever malevolence may have been interred with his bones, much of the evil he promoted lived on.

Early in his work, *The Great Terror*, Robert Conquest traces the roots of Stalinism to the political philosophy of Leninism. All the foundations of a centralized bureaucratic attitude within the Party were established by Lenin, who destroyed any democratic tendencies within the nascent Communist Party.[2] Factions were banned under the Bolshevik leader, making illegal the pursuit of anything but official Party policies. In this, indeed, Stalin did have a political precedent. But there was, according to Conquest, a clear distinction in the justification of terror between Lenin and Stalin. While the terror practiced by Lenin might have been partially justified as the desperate acts of desperate rulers to curb political chaos, Stalin operated in another climate. His was a deliberate, calculated, cold-blooded effort at complete control that was not provoked by events.[3]

Richard Pipes, historian and advisor in Soviet affairs to the National Security Council under President Ronald Reagan, does not subscribe to this nuanced distinction between Lenin and Stalin. Political police and concentration camps were extensively utilized by both rulers for massive repression; the only difference was the scope of their Gulags.[4] Pipes maintains that Lenin's use of mass terror laid the foundations for 20th century mass murder.[5]

When such egregious cruelty succeeds in taking hold of a state, it can only be understood in the context of an interaction of multiple factors. Stalin's autocratic strategy remained constant even as his techniques evolved. Seweryn Bialer provides an elegant analysis of Stalin's developing roles. He describes three major stages in the evolution of Stalinism. The first period was one of consolidation of Bolshevik rule—that is, the shaping of political, administrative and economic institutions as well as policy formulation in the 1920s (NEP era). Bialer categorizes Stalin during this phase as a politician fighting for power in the Communist Party and building organizational bases.[6] During the second stage, the 1929–1938 "revolutions from above," a fundamental transformation of Soviet society took place whereby all institutions of Bolshevism were "radically reshaped." Bialer terms Stalin in this period a "revolutionary transformer and restorer."[7] He labels the third stage "mature Stalinism," when the revolutions from above were over and the political institutions as well as long-range social, economic and cultural policies had been established.[8] He defines Stalin here as a "dictator-administrator." Indeed, terror, bureaucracy and ruthlessness were by this time intrinsic parts of the system. Bialer's criticism of the totalitarian model of Stalinism is that it fails to distinguish its distinct phases. In mature Stalinism, he asserts, terror did not function as a "tool of social change, but as a normal method of governance"9—a persistent "regime of terror." Bialer maintains that the only feasible explanation for the mass terror that gripped the elite and the general population was Stalin's quest for a personal dictatorship; "this characteristic binds and conditions most of the system's other characteristics."10 Bialer's analysis addresses Stalin and his legacy. Let us now consider Stalin and his inheritance.

In his essay "The Marxist Roots of Stalinism," Leszek Kolakowski discusses the relationship of Stalinism to Marxism. The Polish philosopher poses the question of whether the Stalinist ideology and system can be considered a legitimate interpretation of Marxism.11 He raises the possibility that an attempt to implement all the basic values of Marxism would inevitably create a resultant analogous to Stalinism. He answers both questions in the affirmative (p. 284). Stalinism, for Kolakowski, is defined as the period from 1930 to 1953 of one-person despotism in the Soviet Union or as any system that embraces totalitarianism and is based on the state's ownership of the means of production (p. 284). He defines totalitarian as a political system in which all intellectual, political, cultural, and social activities are in the hands of the state and in the service of its goals (p. 285). Individuals are thus the property of the state. Kolakowski asserts that totalitarianism grows and flourishes best in the structure of a socialist economy (p. 285). Though such governments can reshape, rewrite and falsify history, he contends that the "resistance to state ownership of the historical past is an important part of anti-totalitarian movements" (p. 285). Memorial's counter-hegemonic effort to put history back into the hands and mouths of the people is such a movement.

Kolakowski argues that the elements of totalitarianism established by communists during the war became a permanent part of the Soviet social structure. The checks and balances were eliminated by the destruction of the working class as a political force, the abolition of independent trade unions, the abrogation of soviets (councils) as independent forums of popular initiative and the suppression of democracy within the Party (banning of factions) (p. 286). This, of course, was enforced by revolutionary violence. Kolakowski concludes that "the Party was to be taught that ideology is what the leader in any given moment says it is" (p. 287). The people, too, were to learn this lesson.Kolakowski defines mature Stalinism as a society that is fully state-owned, unified by the Party and police. The totalitarian law which hinges on "the arbitrary and changing decisions of executive authorities" creates the grounds by which any citizen at any moment may be considered a criminal, for example, guilty of political crimes as defined in penal codes (p. 287). Kolakowski considers this situation unchanged in the "post-Stalinian" period (pp. 287–288). In totalitarian society, he continues, law becomes a malleable instrument of the head of state. Already under Lenin, the Soviet Union was governed by one leader with limitless power. Soviet society under Stalin was never answerable to the Secret Police but to Stalin himself. He governed the Party, the political machine and the country in that hierarchical order. Reflecting on the universal spying that was encouraged, Kolakowski aptly summarizes the cannibalism of paranoia: "the unattainable ideal of the system seems to have been a situation where all people were at the same time inmates of concentration camps and secret police agents" (p. 289). This provides a sardonic twist to the ideal that each man should be his brother's keeper.

On the issue of the ideologic hegemony as a characteristic of mature Stalinism, Kolakowski describes the contrasting views of Solzhenitsyn and Sakharov. The former maintained that the whole structure of the Soviet state is based on the rule of the false Marxist ideology, which is responsible for all the social and state disasters. Sakharov asserted that ideology is dead and could not thus be a real guiding force in shaping policy (p. 289). Bolshevism, according to Kolakowski, professed itself to be the sole advocate for the working class. Marxist ideology permitted it to be the sole arbiter of the worker's will, even if unenlightened workers were unwilling to accept it. He astutely notes that the ideology contrived by the Soviet state is its only legitimacy. The equation of ideology with Party legitimacy will be further discussed in relation to Gorbachev.

Kolakowski contends that the historical background of Russian totalitarianism was a template for Russian communism, and he wonders if perhaps the whole meaning of "Marxism in Russia ultimately consisted in injecting into a shaky empire fresh ideological blood," allowing it to survive for a while before finally falling apart (p. 290).

Certain precepts of Marxism should be clarified. In a theoretical discussion, Kolakowski dissects Marx's model. He begins with Marxism's assertion that the division of labor results in the alienation of labor (pp. 290–292). A revolutionary process breaks down the structure maintaining this condition and creates a new order in which the social process is subordinated to the collective will of associated individuals (p. 291). He describes Marx's vision of a civilization in which progress would overcome its own destructiveness and the new unity it offered would be based on freedom from wants rather than suppression of needs (p. 292). Communal property would converge individual with universal interests and the distinctions between civil society and the state would be abolished. The Marxist Party as the sole embodiment of truth can then justify a dictatorship over the minds of the people: "Once the spirit of the Party is perfectly incarnated in one leader (as the highest expression of Society's unity), we have the ultimate equation: truth = proletarian consciousness = Marxism = party's ideology = party leaders' idea = chief's decisions" (p. 294). Thus, there is logically nothing un-Marxist in the oft-repeated statement, "Comrade Stalin is never wrong" (p. 294). As for Lenin, Kolakowski asserts that he took Marx's "dictatorship of the proletariat" not for the class content it might have alluded to, but at face value. Lenin's dictatorship was one based on violence and not constrained by law (p. 294).

According to Kolakowski, Soviet ideology had oversimplified Marxism, using it as a tool to build a new society. Since the only tool was a hammer, the government treated everything like a nail. In short, the whole theory of communism was summed up as "the abolition of private property" (p. 296). The state would own the factories and land, society would be liberated, and national hostilities along with class antagonism would inevitably disappear (p. 296). Marx contended that there would be no liberation for human society without the unity that could only be produced by despotism. Destruction of the individual would eliminate the conflicts between the individual and the "whole." Thus, Stalin could be seen as diligently administering a prescription to an ailing nation. Many would think that the cure was worse than the disease. For better or worse, the trajectory that started with Marxism eventuated in Stalinism.

An alternative point of view is presented by Robert Tucker in his essay, "Stalinism as Revolution from Above." He looks to Russian history and argues that Stalinism did not result directly from Leninism. The factors shaping the particular form that the Stalinist phase assumed were the historical heritage, elements of Russia's past that emerged under Stalin, the heritage of Bolshevik revolutionism and the particular personality of Stalin.[12] Tucker views NEP as an interval between two phases of the revolutionary process, 1917–1921 and 1929–1939. Stalin and Stalinism had little trouble appropriating texts in Lenin's writing to justify policies of the revolution from above (p. 90). In some passages, for example, Lenin had stated that the revolution does not end with the Party's seizure of power but with the destruction of the old order from above.

War Communism militarized the revolutionary-political culture of the Bolshevik movement. Thus, many who came of age politically during this period shared Stalin's (and Lenin's) belief in ruthless resort to terror as an instrument of dictatorial rule. Stalin's pursuit of class war against the kulaks, requisitioning their grain and imposing mass collectivization, appealed to the sentiment and enduring strength of War Communism (p. 91).

Tucker does not see an exact analogy between the use of police terror as a prime political instrument under Stalin and the Red Terror of the Civil War period by the Cheka under Lenin. Nor does he find much continuity between Bolshevism and Stalinism. Instead, he considers Stalin's type of terror a reversion to processes seen earlier in Russian history (p. 95).

Likewise, Tucker views Stalin's revolution from above as rooted in precursors in the political culture of Tsarist Russia. Princes and, later, tsars of Muscovy built powerful "military-national" states as a protection against encroaching neighboring states that occupied portions of the territories constituting Kievan Rus (p. 96). Serfdom and the village commune were utilized as instruments of mutual responsibility in order to fulfill state-imposed obligations. The kolkhoz was thus perceived by many Russian peasants as a "revival of serfdom." Indeed, even the internal passport system, binding the peasant to the kolkhoz as it did his ancestors to landed estates, was re-instituted (p. 97). Long before Lenin or Stalin, Peter the Great used forced labor camps for industrial projects, but on a much smaller scale than the Soviets. After 1939, Tucker points out, we can also see a return to pre-revolutionary patterns in art, education, law and family. In fact, he adds, "there were distinctly reactionary or counter-revolutionary overtones in the revolution from above" (pp. 98–99).

Stalin took Ivan the Terrible's 16th century purge as a model for his own Great Purge. Stalin's purge aimed at a restoration of absolute autocracy, a continuation of the process toward a "neo-tsarist" version of the compulsory-service state, properly called "totalitarian" (p. 100). Tucker highlights an ironic juxtaposition: "The Stalinist stage of the Revolution yielded . . . an amalgamated Stalinist Soviet culture that paradoxically involved at once the full-scale sovietization of Russian society and the Russification of the Soviet culture" (p. 102). By 1945, the war had reinforced previous tendencies of Great Russian nationalism, militarism and official anti-Semitism (p. 105). Reversion to pre-revolutionary Russian themes has occurred at other times and in similar forms in Soviet history. Then, as in the recent past, it manifested itself at a time when the strength of the Soviet state was faltering.

In a broad-sweeping article entitled "Bolshevism and Stalinism," Stephen Cohen examines various interpretations of Stalinism and expresses his dissatisfaction with the continuity theory. For many, he acknowledges, Stalinism was the inevitable outcome of Bolshevism. No significant political or ideological distinctions are made between the two. Cohen argues that such a perspective is too undifferentiated and obfuscates the study of Stalinism as a distinct phenomenon with its own history, rules, political dynamics and social consequences.[13] Echoing Trotsky, many within the political Left even saw Stalinism as Bolshevism's "Thermidorian" negation and betrayal. Stalinism, Cohen asserts, must be examined against the background of the social and political circumstances of the time, along with Stalin's unique personality. Some approaches are not very enlightening. Cohen quotes one analyst's tautological perspective: "Russian communism had to turn out as it has because it now can be seen to have, in fact, turned out as it has" (p. 6)!

Cohen points out that, basically, Robert Daniels, Zbigniew Brzezinski, Robert H. McNeal, Adam B. Ulam and Arthur P. Mendel all argue in favor of the continuity theory, that is, "deterministically." In brief, this position contends that Stalinism (including its manifestation from 1928 to 1939) eventuated from the ideological, programmatic and organizational nature of original Bolshevism (p. 7). Cohen finds this perspective problematic because it conceives of all of Bolshevik and Soviet history and policies before 1929 as simply the "ante-chamber" of Stalinism. The main disagreements, he adds, focus largely on whether Stalinism began in 1902 with Lenin's "What Is To Be Done," in October 1917 with the Bolshevik revolution, in January 1918 with the abolishment of the Constituent Assembly, in 1921 with the ban on party factions, or in 1923 with Trotsky's first defeat (p. 10). Scholars in the 1960s, Cohen tells us, began to put Stalinism against a historical background in the context of Russia's backwardness but in essence they were reformulating rather than challenging the continuity theory (p. 10).

Though Bolshevism was an authoritarian movement, Cohen argues that a qualitative and quantitative distinction must be made between Soviet authoritarianism before and after 1929. He adds that "excesses were the essence of historical Stalinism"—excess of nationalism, bureaucratization, lack of democracy, censorship, police repression (pp. 12–13). Indeed, Stalinism is defined by its excesses.

Cohen, distinguishes at least three stages of Stalinism: 1929–1933, social upheaval and the formative period of Stalinism as a system; 1934–1935, interregnum wherein future policy was contested within the leadership; 1936–1939, the "final triumph of Stalinism over the Bolshevik tradition and the political completion of revolution from above" (p. 24). The expansion of police repression, security forces and forced labor camps of 1929–1933, Cohen contends, were preparations for 1936–1939. Cohen differentiates Leninism from Bolshevism, the latter being a much larger phenomenon that was also shaped by other leaders (p. 13). Like others, he describes how the Civil War impacted on the Bolshevik outlook and militarized the Party (p. 15). Cohen does recognize that the growing centralization and bureaucratization of the Party after 1917 promoted authoritarianism in the one-party system, and that Stalin's early stratagems in the NEP were radically unlike Stalinism. He further maintains that after 1929, the Bolshevik programmatic alternative to Stalinism was Bukharinism (see Chapter 1). Cohen asserts that the period 1929–1933 constituted a radical departure from Bolshevik thinking and concludes that "these years of 'revolution from above' were, historically and programmatically, the birth period of Stalinism. From the first great discontinuity others would follow" (p. 24).

The past few years have permitted a great number of opinions to be voiced on this issue in the former Soviet Union. In *Glasnost in Action*, Alec Nove surveys a number of Soviet discussions in progress during 1989 appearing in articles that debate the themes of Stalin and Stalinism. Gavriil Popov discusses the "economic-political essence of Stalinism" and maintains that several features had to co-exist for it to function: the despot himself, the "subsystem of fear" (terror), the tasks imposed by the despot and managed by centralized administrative order, and the loyal executants dedicated to both Stalin and the cause.[14]

Mikhail Gefter asserts that Stalin deliberately set up policies and strategies that made it seem that he was essential to the security of the system: "Waging a war against a large part of his own people, eliminating alternative policies and the advocates of such policies . . . creating the atmosphere of a beleaguered fortress menaced by spies and saboteurs, all were part of the act."[15] Instead of promoting a process of normalization that might have rendered him unnecessary, Stalin launched the Terror. Stalin's provocation of "permanent civil war," according to the Soviet historian, was his most significant personal contribution to Stalinism.[16] Gefter continues that Lenin's line of thought offered alternatives—NEP, for example. But the very ambiguities of NEP weakened its ability to effectively oppose Stalin. Still, Nove adds, letters to the press have confirmed the existence not only of a Stalinshchina but also of a Leninshchina. They support the view that "Stalin was, after all, a follower of Lenin, that the real 'catastrophe' was the October revolution itself."[17] But Gefter contends that ultimately Stalin "caused so much blood to flow, he is linked with blood so closely in all his actions, that it destroys all rational explanation, both of him as a person and of our history."[18] Stalin's peer was not a colorless bureaucratic murderer such as Eichmann ("the banality of evil"), but Adolf Hitler. He was, like his Nazi counterpart, a paranoid madman who seized control of the state apparatus, stripped it of its corrective checks and balances and destroyed its human resources. He had met the enemy, and it was his own people.

Gefter finally discusses the perplexing question of Stalin's reputed popularity. He explains how some maintain that the cult of personality was organized and created from both above and below. In the hierarchically organized Russian society, people are inclined to look to leaders for governance. People needed a leader to look up to.[19] The more desperate the situation, the greater the need for leadership. This may be one explanation of the paradoxical phenomenon of the patriotic loyalty during World War II, even from those who were recently released from camps or less recently victims of collectivization. Even today many again call for a "leader like Stalin," a strong and stable hand at the helm to get the former Soviet nation back on course. Whenever fear and vulnerability grip the populace, if they cannot find security in the cultural system (political or religious), they tend to turn to the strong man with simple answers to complex questions.

The characteristic elements of Stalinism have been well described by historians and political scientists. To reiterate Popov's analysis, these are: terror, bureaucratization, the ruthless leader himself and loyal executants and believers. In fact, these were all characteristics of Lenin's rule as well. The fact that they were also components in the Marxist system suggests a definite connection between Marxism and Stalinism. It is also clear that these features of authoritarianism did not manifest themselves in Russia only for the first time under the Soviet state. Whatever its roots, its legacy can still be seen in the Soviet system. Any attempt to alter the present necessitates an understanding of the forces that shaped and are still shaping it. This is the mandate of Memorial. Who could more appropriately pose the questions and seek the answers than the group that remembers the victims of Stalinism?

NOTES

1. Seweryn Bialer, *Stalin's Successors* (Cambridge: Cambridge University Press, 1980), p. 8.

2. Robert Conquest, *The Great Terror* (Middlesex, England: Penguin Books, 1968), p. 25.

3. Ibid., pp. 376–377.

4. *NRC Handelsblad* (Rotterdam), 8 December 1990.

5. Ibid.

6. Bialer, p. 9.

7. Ibid.

8. Ibid., p. 10.

9. Ibid., p. 12.

10. Ibid., p. 27.

11. Leszek Kolakowski, "The Marxist Roots of Stalinism," in *Stalinism: Essays in Historical Interpretation*, ed. Robert C. Tucker (New York: W. W. Norton & Company, 1977), p. 284.

12. Robert C. Tucker, "Stalinism as Revolution from Above," in *Stalinism: Essays in Historical Interpretation*, ed. Robert C. Tucker (New York: W. W. Norton & Company, 1977), p. 78.

13. Stephen F. Cohen, "Bolshevism and Stalinism," in *Stalinism*, ed. Robert C. Tucker, p. 4.

14. Alec Nove, *Glasnost in Action* (Boston: Unwin Hyman, 1989), p. 23.

15. Ibid., p. 25.

16. Ibid., p. 26.

17. Ibid., p. 31.

18. Ibid., p. 27.

19. Ibid., p. 29.

CHAPTER 3 _____

The Rediscovery of Soviet History

If we conceptualize history as a dialectic process, then the excessive repression of the Stalinist system would eventually have evoked a corrective force such as Memorial. How long Stalinism could have continued on its course of unchecked repression is an open question, but it is certain that Memorial could not have come into existence in its present form and at this time until the repressive apparatus had begun to weaken.

The first official effort toward de-Stalinization may be marked by the report Khrushchev delivered to the Central Committee at the XX Party Congress on February 14, 1956. In it, Khrushchev cautiously criticized Stalin and alluded to the "cult of personality." At the same time, however, covering his conservative bases (Khrushchev could hardly ignore them, considering his own background as a protégé of Kaganovich), he credited Stalin with crushing the "enemies of the people."[1] With some difficulty, a commission was established to investigate these matters. Khrushchev's second report, a secret speech on Stalin's crimes, was presented to a closed session of the congress. Still proceeding cautiously, this report focused on crimes committed against Party members loyal to Stalin and the general Party line rather than those against oppositionists. Though pages of the report were leaked, for personal and political reasons, Khrushchev was not yet ready to publicize the plight of what Michel Heller and Aleksandr Nekrich call "the principal victims of the regime: the millions of ordinary Soviet citizens."[2] Still, even in its muted form, the report was a "bombshell."[3]

In the climate of the times, simply calling attention to the dragon was a bold venture. It would remain for others to challenge the dragon in its lair. In an emotional diatribe that was part confessional, part disclaimer, part accusation, Khrushchev disclosed the Stalinist mechanisms of terror, denounced the system of arbitrariness and the "cult of personality" and indicated that Stalin was behind Kirov's murder. He depicted a governmental system whose modus operandi included criminal acts, lawlessness, mass murder, incompetent leadership and a systematic cover-up through the falsification of history.[4] Subsequently, the disclosure spread to every Party organization in the country. Heated debates arose centering first on Stalin and then even on the Soviet system itself. Thousands of prisoners had been released since 1953, but in the year of the congress, 1956, such efforts were accelerated. The "Terror Decree" of December 1, 1934, was abolished in April of that year.[5] The rehabilitation commissions that were set up freed a great majority of surviving prisoners and posthumously rehabilitated many victims. Significantly, this rehabilitation did not extend to opposition leaders.[6]

The road to reform was still a treacherous footpath. Conquest asserts that Kolyma had changed little by 1956.[7] Although democratic movements experienced an upsurge, Soviet and foreign Stalinists, fearing their own culpability in the crimes of Stalinism, united against the reformers. Subsequently, a resolution "On Overcoming the Cult of Personality and Its Consequences" was adopted at a CPSU (Communist Party of the Soviet Union) Central Committee session of June 30, 1956.[8] It praised Stalin as a theoretician and organizer and attempted to justify his fight against oppositionists. Stalin's abuse of power was decried, but blame was deflected from the socialist system that supported it to his "personal defects."[9]

While conservative forces may have been mollified by this, the voices of reform were becoming strident. Reactions to the official admission of Stalin's crimes were less muted in the Soviet satellites. There were uprisings in Poland and Hungary, the latter leading to Soviet intervention.[10] Though Khrushchev was clearly trying to disengage himself from a failed system, he was not ready or able to tolerate its overthrow. When the throne falls, those who stand closest are in danger of being crushed.

Khrushchev's efforts were directed more toward modifying and therefore stabilizing the system rather than correcting its fundamental flaws. He improved the standard of living by reducing taxes and permitted disability compensation, but he also introduced new forms of political repression like the 1957 campaign against "parasites" (often targeted at writers and poets). The "parasite" law, for example, was used against

Joseph Brodsky in 1964.[11] Boris Pasternak, who was awarded the Nobel Prize for Literature in 1958, was forced to decline it for fear of exile from his country. But the genie of private protest could not be forced back into the bureaucratic bottle. The Pasternak affair awakened public opinion, as witnessed by sympathetic letters of support that poured in from all over the world.[12] The groundswell of criticism was also being carried back to the populace by political prisoners returning from camps and by their fellow prisoners politicized by their incarceration.

Khrushchev's efforts in the legislative arena were, at best, ambivalent. In December 1958 a new decree on state crimes abolished Article 58 (on "counter-revolutionary crimes"), but severe punishment was still employed for all forms of action, organization or discussion hostile to the government.[13] Vyshinsky's confession theories were denounced, though the method was not abandoned. Moreover, a decree by the Supreme Soviet on May 5, 1961, provided the death penalty for "some acts of aggression against administration" in the camps.[14] Much was still left to the discretion of the authorities.

Several attempts were made to recover the historical truth of the Stalinist Terror, but they were met with determined resistance. The publication in 1962 in the Soviet Union of Alexander Solzhenitsyn's *One Day in the Life of Ivan Denisovich*, a former prisoner's account of a typical day in Soviet labor camp, had Khrushchev's personal approval over the objections of ideologists. It received an enthusiastic response from the "nonconformist" sectors of society but earned the enmity of Stalinists; consequently, official persecution of Solzhenitsyn began a year after publication.[15] Some political prisoners were given the status of common criminals for "dissemination of fabrications discrediting the Soviet state and social system."[16] Others were "treated" in either "special" or "ordinary" psychiatric institutions, thus relocating the failures of the political system from the institutions of state to the psyche of the individual so that the Soviet system could deny its own structural derangement.

In October 1961 at the XXII Party Congress, Khrushchev was emboldened to make more specific claims against a group that took part in an "anti-Party" campaign in the late 1950s. Signatures of members of Stalin's inner circle—Molotov, Kaganovich, Malenkov, Voroshilov—were shown on death penalties for even the wives of "enemies of the people."[17] The Congress, consequently, voted unanimously in favor of both removing Stalin's body from the Lenin Mausoleum and building a memorial to Stalin's victims.[18] The memorial was not built, but Stalin's body was transferred from the mausoleum to the base of the Kremlin wall. After this took place a poem written by Yevgeny Yevtushenko called "The Heirs to

Stalin" was published in *Pravda*. Its words express an issue central to Memorial:

> To double
>   To triple
>   The guard at this slab
> So that Stalin may not rise,
> And with Stalin
>   The past . . .
> We rooted him
>   Out of the Mausoleum
>   But how to root Stalin
>   Out of Stalin's heirs?[19]

Despite the removal of Stalin's body, Khrushchev's de-Stalinization campaign remained cautious and ambivalent. His speech on the tenth anniversary of Stalin's death retained the 1956 CPSU Central Committee image of Stalin as the hero—with, however, inevitable human foibles. He praised Stalin's struggle against opposition elements and attributed Stalin's mistakes to his "overly suspicious nature and persecution mania."[20]

Khrushchev's own economic and political failings were not as tolerantly overlooked by his comrades. His errors of "commission and omission"[21] undermined his authority, weakened his ability to overcome Stalinist forces and eventually contributed to his downfall. In his attempt to work within the system in order to modify the system, Khrushchev can be said to have laid the groundwork for both "de-Stalinization" and "re-Stalinization." The strong Stalinist elements that brought him to power and on which he still had to rely for governance gave him little leeway for change.

Indeed, the primal fault of Stalinism for the Soviets, like the primal fault of the Third Reich for the Germans, was a historical reality that both postwar governments would have to resolve. But there was a difference. It was politically easier for a postwar Germany to denounce Hitler because he had been defeated and he could clearly be blamed for defeat. By contrast, the still entrenched Stalinists could claim victory in the "Great Patriotic War." It was the Allies, not the Germans, who dethroned Hitler. The transformation from war hero to domestic monster would require a delicate political dynamic for the Soviets.

Gorbachev's statement after the XXVII Party Congress that there should no longer be blank spots and forgotten names[22] in history and literature[23] was a bold but, in retrospect, unavoidable change in Soviet politics. Two key speeches by Khrushchev and Gorbachev, Party leaders, separated by three decades, signaled the official recognition that moving forward would first necessitate looking backward. Stalin would first have to be demythologized. *His* story would have to be discredited before competing stories could be heard. Defeat of another kind—economic defeat by Western democracies—also played a key role in the disparagement of Stalinism. "Before he can introduce a market economy," said one journalist referring to Gorbachev, "he must discredit the Stalinist system of central planning."[24]

The situation that Mikhail S. Gorbachev had to confront by the time of his speech on November 2, 1987, commemorating the 70th anniversary of the October Revolution was that two truths co-existed simultaneously in the Soviet Union: the dogmatic, official, bureaucratic truth and the unofficial one that existed in the consciousness of the people.[25] The former was loudly trumpeted through all the Party organs on the political stage; the latter, unutterable, was a whisper that rippled through the audience and would not go away. Gorbachev began by praising Khrushchev but ultimately buried him. Gorbachev lauded Khrushchev's program that led to the rehabilitation of thousands of innocent victims, but he added that the process of restoring justice was not completed and, in fact, had practically come to a halt by the mid-1960s. Gorbachev went on to say that in the last years under Brezhnev, the search for ways to move forward was hindered by clinging to old formulas that did not relate to reality and, additionally, led to a gap between word and deed.[26]

Gorbachev's admission that mass repression of "thousands" of Party and non-Party members had taken place under Stalin was a disappointment for many who knew this to be a grossly understated estimate. But it might be argued that this statement was, nevertheless, as monumental as Khrushchev's revelations at the XX and XXII Party Congresses, because by reopening the subject Gorbachev allowed people to go out and discover the real numbers. The numbers would speak for themselves so that the leadership at the time would not have to take responsibility for some of the jarring disclosures. There are, however, frequent reminders in this speech that Gorbachev, as the general secretary of the Communist Party of the Soviet Union and as a committed socialist, was constantly performing a balancing act between the pressure to promote democratization and the need to maintain the Party. Evolution, not revolution, is what he was calling for. Gorbachev did not express total condemnation of Stalin, maintaining that the historical truth should include Stalin's accomplishments in the "struggle for socialism," which must not be forgotten.[27] However, he asserted that documents had proven that Stalin did know of the arbitrariness, that the cult of personality was not at all unavoidable, and that the cult in itself was a deviation from the principles of socialism.[28] In effect he was saying not that socialism was bad but that Stalin was a bad Socialist. Gorbachev added that a commission was formed to study new and already known facts and documents in connection with these issues.[29] Though this position did not go far enough for the reformers, the official sanction helped to "legitimize" Memorial's cause and further its signature campaign.

Gorbachev's support for uncovering the historical truth was again reflected at the 19th Party Conference in June 1988. By this time the Supreme Soviet had received over 10,000 signatures (collected by Memorial) in Moscow alone[30] and a total of 20,000 from thirty other cities calling for the erection of a monument and memorial center in honor of victims of the Stalinist purges. In a closing speech, Gorbachev announced that a monument would be built in Moscow to restore justice to the victims of lawlessness, adding that it was the Party's "political and moral duty."[31] This, in turn, allowed establishment liberals to join—and later lead—Memorial.[32]

The rediscovery of history under Gorbachev resulted in great numbers of rehabilitations of Party and non-Party members. By August 1988, thousands of victims—highly placed oppositionists, peasants, workers and ordinary citizens—of Stalin's terror were rehabilitated as a result of the findings of the governmental commission set up in November 1987. Their families also received rehabilitation, which meant restoration of civil rights and some compensation. The commission concluded that the personal fault of Stalin and his close advisors in large-scale lawless repression was horrendous.[33] Two years later, in August 1990, Gorbachev cleared the way for the rehabilitation of millions of victims, characterizing Stalin's crimes as "mass repression, arbitrariness and lawlessness."[34] In the meantime, Soviet as well as Western historical texts and hitherto forbidden literature such as Solzhenitsyn's *Gulag Archipelago* (presented in lengthy installments in *Novyi Mir* in 1989) were being published in the Soviet Union. The Soviet culpability in such incidents as the Katyn forest massacre of Polish officers was officially acknowledged, and Memorial was able to create a joint exhibition on this theme with the Krakow Museum on the History of Photography in April 1990.

Inevitably, perhaps, Gorbachev's de-Stalinization program had its ideologic limits. Lenin and the Red Terror under Lenin were taboo topics and would remain so as long as Lenin was deified. Andrei Sakharov's arguments in 1988 for the exoneration of victims of Khrushchev and Brezhnev (and, we might infer, Gorbachev) touched on a delicate issue for Gorbachev.[35] Great numbers of posthumous and other rehabilitations of these victims and their families took place under the last Soviet leader. This even included people who were still voicing dissent. However, Gorbachev could not sanction a wholesale condemnation of the crimes committed under Soviet rule, because he was concerned that it might destabilize his position as well as that of his Party. This may be an important reason why the All-Union Memorial did not attain official registration until as late as 1991. More attention will be devoted to this problem in chapter 8. Analysis of the stance taken by Gorbachev in the post-Soviet era regarding crimes that occurred under Communism is beyond the scope of this work. But it is worth considering. In his time in office, even a wholesale condemnation of such crimes might not have saved Gorbachev. Still, in the post-Soviet Russia of 1992, Gorbachev's stance remained steadfast although his position did not. The former Soviet leader turned down an invitation to attend a trial on the constitutionality of a ban of the Communist Party.[36] Nor would he lend his support to criminal charges against the Party. Gorbachev claimed that such a trial would lead to a schism in society that would further destabilize the country.[37] He was right about the risks of destabilization. He was wrong in his assessment that it could be prevented. The Soviet *system's* deficiency of self-corrective awareness and action doomed it to self-destruction.

NOTES

1. Michel Heller and Aleksandr Nekrich, *Utopia in Power* (London: Hutchinson, 1986), p. 530.
2. Ibid., p. 531.
3. Ibid.
4. Ibid.
5. Robert Conquest, *The Great Terror* (Middlesex, England: Penguin Books, 1968), p. 686.
6. Heller and Nekrich, p. 526.
7. Conquest, p. 687.
8. Heller and Nekrich, p. 533.
9. Ibid.
10. Ibid., p. 538.
11. Ibid., pp. 560–561.
12. Ibid., p. 580.
13. Conquest, p. 686.
14. Ibid., p. 688.
15. Heller and Nekrich, p. 588.
16. Ibid., p. 589.
17. Ibid., p. 597.

18. *Guardian* (London), 23 June 1988.

19. Yevgeny Yevtushenko, "The Heirs to Stalin," *The Current Digest of the Soviet Press* 14, no. 40 (1972): 50.

20. Heller and Nekrich, p. 599.

21. Ibid.

22. Gorbachev's personal family history also included one such name. In December 1991 it was revealed that one of Gorbachev's grandfathers was a kulak.

23. *Gorbatschows historische Rede* (Munich: Wilhelm Heyne Verlag, 1987), p. 8.

24. *Washington Post*, 27 December 1988.

25. *Gorbatschows historische Rede*, p. 8.

26. Ibid., p. 67.

27. Ibid., p. 54.

28. Ibid.

29. Ibid., p. 56.

30. *UPI*, 22 June 1988.

31. *Reuters*, 4 July 1988.

32. *Nyeformaly: Civil Society in the USSR*, A Helsinki Watch Report (New York: Helsinki Watch, 1990), p. 62.

33. *Reuters*, 20 August 1988.

34. *NRC Handelsblad* (Rotterdam), 14 August 1990.

35. *Daily Telegraph* (London), 31 October 1988.

36. *International Herald Tribune*, 8 July 1992.

37. *Reuters/AFP*, 8 July 1992.

The Igarka-Salekhard railway, one of the last main forced labor projects of Stalin. The railway was never completed and the camps were abandoned immediately following Stalin's death. Photo by Alexander Vologodsky.

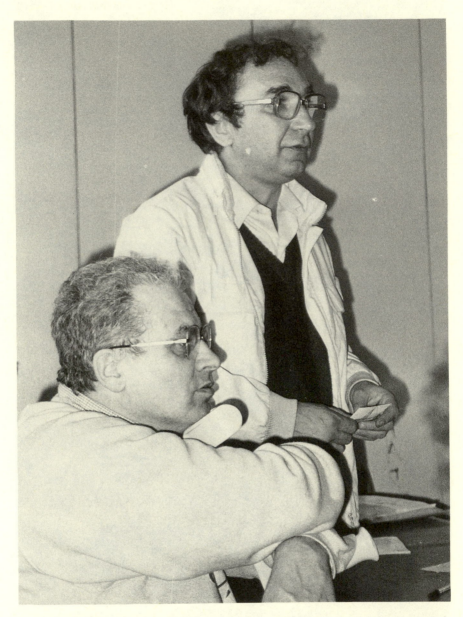

Arseny Roginsky, member of Memorial's Scientific Council, and Veniamin Iofe (left), co-chairman of its Leningrad chapter, at a Memorial Seminar on "Maps of the Gulag," April 19, 1990. Photo by Rob Knijff.

Defunct train left at the Igarka-Salekhard railway. Photo by Alexander Vologodsky.

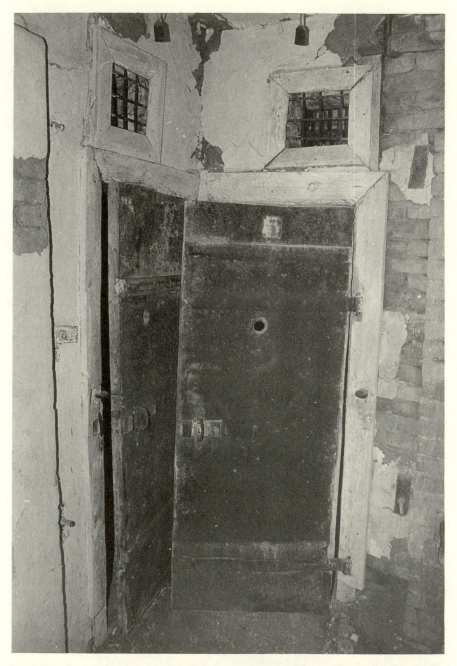

Punishment cell in one of the camps along the railway. Photo by Alexander Vologodsky.

Prisoners' barracks in one of the camps along the Igarka-Salekhard railway. Photo by Alexander Vologodsky.

Prisoner's grave, usually marked with only a number. Photo by Alexander Vologodsky.

Memorial demonstration encircling KGB headquarters in Moscow on the "Day of the Political Prisoners," October 30, 1989. Photo by Alexander Vologodsky.

Demonstration of Sverdlovsk Memorial. From left to right: "From an empire to a union of free peoples; Stalinists want blood; No fascism!" Still from Sverdlovsk Film Studio, Boris Kustov.

Memorial has created an exhibition called "The country as a GULAG, the GULAG as a country," of which they consider this image a prime example. The majority of such structures, built from the 1920s to the 1950s, were constructed by the prisoners of Stalin's labor camps and can therefore be considered symbolic of the architecture of the Soviet State. Photo by Alexander Vologodsky.

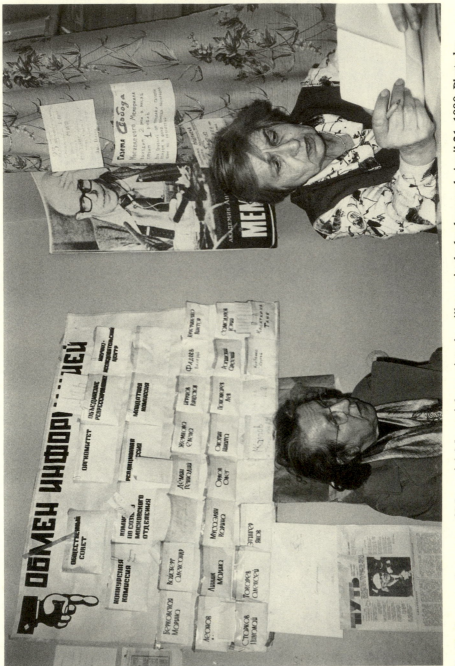

Inside the reception room of Memorial. Memorial associates' mailboxes in the background. April 21, 1990. Photo by Rob Knijff.

In the absence of official registration, Memorial's files were kept in various private apartments, such as this one belonging to one of the organization's leaders, Nikita Okhotin. April 20, 1990. Photo by Rob Knijff.

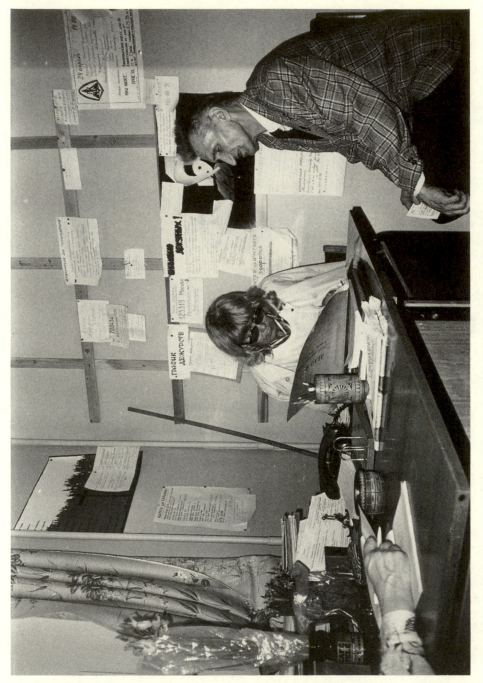

Legal Advice Day in the Memorial reception room, April 1990. Photo by Rob Knijff.

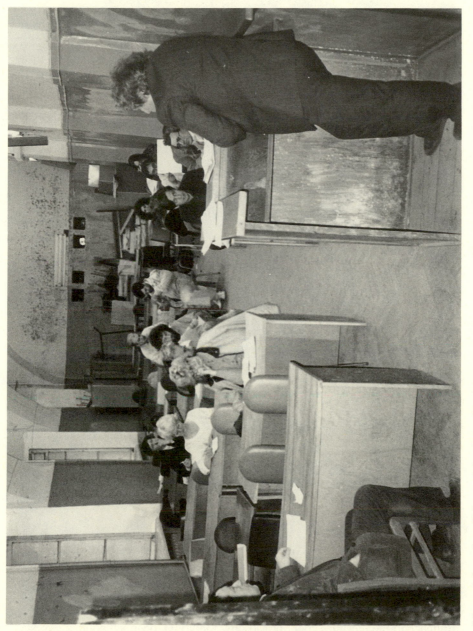

Memorial seminar "Maps of the Gulag" in historical archive institute, April 19, 1990. Photo by Rob Knijff.

Entrance to the reception room of Moscow Memorial, open ten hours a day, six days a week. Those who were repressed (and/or their family members) come here to relate their tales, offer documents and receive moral and social support. April 21, 1990. Photo by Rob Knijff.

Memorial's monument to the victims of Stalinism on former Dzerzhinsky Square, a stone from the Solovetsky labor camps, November 7 (Revolution Day), 1991. Photo by Rob Kniff.

Fallen statue of Stalin, Central House of Artists, Moscow, July 1992. Photo by Mikhail B. Gnedovsky.

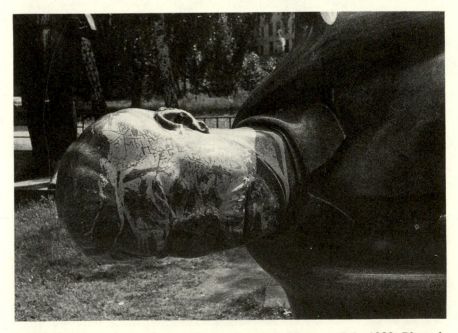

Detail of Stalin's head, Central House of Artists, Moscow, July 1992. Photo by Mikhail B. Gnedovsky.

At work in the Memorial office in Moscow, August 25, 1992. Photo by Nanci Adler.

PART II _____

THE EMERGENCE AND EVOLUTION OF MEMORIAL

It is difficult to define the contours of Memorial, because of its unofficial origins and its multifaceted activities. What we find when we examine the history of Memorial is the development of the organization along various lines: as a historical-enlightenment society, as a human rights movement, as a social organization and as a political organization. It was the interaction and combination of all these forces that shaped the form and function of Memorial. A chronological examination of Memorial's history, with these themes in mind, may be the clearest way to understand how Memorial developed.

For purposes of discussion, it is useful to divide Memorial's course of development into three phases, which are described in the next three chapters. The first stage, 1987–1988, encompasses the signature campaign, the 70th anniversary of the revolution, the 19th Party Conference and the "Week of Conscience." The second period, 1988–1989, includes Memorial's struggle against official hindrance and the Founding Conference. This event, which established a charter, resolutions and basic moral principles, will be given special attention here because it is essential to understanding the philosophy of Memorial. In the third phase, the aftermath of the Founding Conference, 1989–1990, the movement spread as local divisions emerged in cities all over the Soviet Union, a monument to the victims of totalitarianism was erected in Moscow, and Memorial became more involved in political issues.

CHAPTER 4 _____

1987–1988: Gaining Support

The de-Stalinization from above was accompanied by a parallel process from below. Already in the summer of 1987, some people were setting their own course of de-Stalinization, testing the limits of glasnost.[1] The period from August through December 1987 is of special importance because it reveals much about the mission and methods of both Memorial and Soviet officialdom. In August 1987, a group in Moscow assembled as an initiative group dedicated to establishing a monument to the victims of repression. During a discussion at this meeting, they decided to call themselves "Memorial." They then proceeded to send materials on their project to Soviet press agencies, the newspaper *Moskovskiye Novosti* and the journal *Ogonyok*. The group proclaimed the principles of openness and legality. From the very beginning, Memorial emphasized the fact that their activity was in accordance with Soviet law and that they were not an underground organization, but one that adheres to the spirit and letter of the Soviet Constitution. This is explicitly stated in the Charter. There is historical precedent in referring to the rule of law. "Respect the Constitution" could be seen on posters in Pushkin Square a few months prior to the Sinyavsky and Daniel trial (see Epilogue).[2]

At a meeting in October 1987, Memorial formulated a petition that requested the Supreme Soviet to permit the creation of a memorial to the victims of lawlessness and political terror. Armed with this petition, group members began to collect signatures of support from institutions, organizations and various enterprises.[3] By the end of that month, Western newspapers began reporting on Memorial's activities for the first time.

This coincided with Gorbachev's November 2 anniversary speech in which he showed sympathy for Stalin's victims. Newspapers were now freer to write about such activities, because they fit the spirit of the times.

In mid-November, the signature drive was directed at the general public as the campaign was conducted on the Arbat in Moscow. After one day at this post, six members of the initiative group—D. N. Leonov, L. A. Ponomarev, V. A. Kuzin, Y. P. Skubko, Y. V. Samodurov, and A. D. Vaisberg—were, according to *Russkaya Mysl*, "groundlessly detained by the . . . police . . . with unprovoked application of force."[4] Each was fined fifty rubles for "malicious disobedience of law and violation of social order."[5] M. Y. Kovalenko, a member of the initiative group, sent a letter to Solomentsev, chairman of the commission on rehabilitation of the Central Committee CPSU, calling for the immediate release of his companions. The posters that were confiscated were liberally sprinkled with liberal quotes from Gorbachev speeches. Both in the beginning and later, Memorial explicitly emphasized its policy of adhering to Soviet law and making sure that the authorities did the same.

The following day Leonov and Samodurov continued their collection of signatures in front of the Central House of Artists and were again detained by the police, but were released after an hour. They then sent a petition of protest to the Moscow procurator requesting an investigation into these illegal activities of the authorities. On November 21, a little more than a week after the first signature campaign, yet another signature drive was broken up by the authorities. On November 25 the police made a surprise raid on Kovalenko's apartment and implied that the procurator was involved. Kovalenko was interrogated to find out why he was part of the initiative group. He explained that he was convinced of society's need to know the historical truth, the conditions, causes and mechanisms of the political repression of the Stalinist era. Moreover, Kovalenko declared his determination to see that such illegal and bureaucratic arbitrariness would not happen again. The irony of the situation seems to have been lost on the police. The authorities characterized Memorial's ideas as adventuristic and declared that "the people do not need Memorial."[6] In addition, the authorities threatened to charge them with violation of social order. Kovalenko challenged the plainclothes policeman's authority to speak for the people and added that the collection of signatures was a better way of monitoring society's attitudes toward Memorial's ideas than an interrogation by the police. The police paid a similar visit to Kuzin, but he was not at home to play host.

A pattern of intimidation was clear. Every time Memorial tried to gather signatures, members were taken to police headquarters and interrogated.

Veiled threats were made to Ponomarev, a scientist, and Samodurov, a candidate of geological mineralogy, regarding their work. Upon leaving the station, the police chief mockingly bid them "Good-bye, Vaisbergs,"[7] a generic reference to Jews. Such remarks are typical of one kind of intimidation that Memorial encounters. Conservatives have tried to side-step the issues raised by Memorial by, among other things, appealing to a reservoir of anti-Semitism in the population. In comparison with the general population, Jews are statistically overrepresented in Memorial, although Memorial is not connected with any specifically Jewish causes, unless we consider the questioning of arbitrary authority a Jewish cause.

After the Moscow section of Memorial's initiative group had openly declared their goals, they met on December 11, 1987, with the Moscow City Committee of the CPSU, but there was no meeting of minds. They were told by the committee that the members of the initiative group were viewed as "helpers in the carrying out of the party line in life" and that the committee was "preliminarily acquainted with the biographies of each of them."[8] The committee said that they agreed, in principle, to the idea of erecting a monument. However, they found that the initiative group was premature in raising the question since the Party's immediate priorities lay in economic reforms. Only after such reforms, they contended, could the people take part in social initiatives. They added ominously that the creation of a monument would distract people from higher priorities and that they considered the gathering of signatures to be "political agitation," a code word for legal culpability. The Memorial group, after expressing their doubts about the logic of this interpretation, explained their own position—namely, that economic reform and democratization are interrelated processes. They wondered aloud how the erection of a monument could hinder the process of reform. The Memorial members continued that the form of the remembrance should be discussed by society and be the result of an initiative from below. They chastised the authorities for their dismissal of the sentiments of public opinion as reflected in the signatures. Memorial then asked the Moscow City Committee to cease the illegal actions toward them, prohibit such behavior by the police and the KGB, and work with the group in a manner that the committee and stated public policy deemed acceptable. The City Committee responded that they considered Memorial's form of activity illegal and that cooperation on their part would be out of the question. The committee recommended that Memorial study material on the Stalinist era in public libraries. Nevertheless, Memorial members stood their ground and emphasized that they had the right to act within the proper interpretation of the framework of the law.

At the manifest level, the erection of a monument to the dead would seem a commonplace, even sentimental gesture, which the government would be frivolous to oppose. After all, there are monuments to the dead all over the former Soviet Union. But these are no ordinary dead. The latent function of the monument, known but unstated, roiled in the consciousness of both Memorial and the intransigent officialdom. There was literary as well as historical precedent for this apprehension. Mark Antony had come simply, as he declared, not to praise Caesar but to bury him. But how can one preside over a burial without a eulogy for the deceased? And what is a eulogy if not a recounting of the meaning of their life and their death? It was, then, not the silent stone monument that troubled the authorities. They correctly saw it as a ghost carved in stone. A ghost that would haunt their nights and trouble their days.

By the beginning of January 1988 the initiative group of Memorial had collected about 1,300 signatures in Moscow alone. Similar activities were being carried out in other cities all over the country. In Leningrad, an initiative group created in July 1987 conducted signature campaigns at meetings, concerts and exhibitions. They had gathered about 1,000 signatures by January. Both *Literaturnaya Gazeta* and *Russkaya Mysl* proudly announced that the signatories included such prominent perestroika figures as Ales Adamovich, Vyacheslav Kondratev, Mikhail Shatrov and Yuri Afanasyev, among many others.[9]

Responding to a liberalization of official policies, the spring of 1988 witnessed an upsurge in the number of informal groups (over 30,000).[10] They represented a broad range of causes with names like "Democracy and Humanism," "Perestroika '88," "Perestroika-Democracy," the "Club of Social Initiative," "Freedom of Emigration for All" and, of course, "Memorial." Constituents from many of these groups could be seen at various demonstrations promoting democracy, but the press reports show that Memorial was always a common denominator. One such event took place on March 5, 1988, the 35th anniversary of Stalin's death. Over six hundred people gathered for a forty-five minute silent march through Moscow to commemorate Stalin's victims and to protest repression.[11] Many of these "new era dissidents," though trying to work within the constraints of Gorbachev's glasnost and democratization, had only days before protested against the bureaucracy that Stalin instituted and that, they asserted, remained deeply ingrained in the Soviet system.[12] That demonstration was broken up by the police. This was a silent demonstration without signs. It was "against all repressions and not just those of Stalin," explained Lev Timofeyev, who was released after two years of a seven-year prison sentence he had received under Gorbachev.[13] His crime was anti-Soviet agitation and propaganda. Despite the fact that the march was dispersed, the event was considered a victory for the sponsoring organizations. It established a precedent for a manner of protest that would later be repeated.

In early May 1988, a three-day conference of informal groups took place. One hundred representatives from eight Soviet cities gathered in Moscow. Militiamen appeared on the third day to break up the event. They arrested twenty-four people for trying to organize an opposition party.[14] then an illegal act under Article 6 of the Soviet Constitution. Though Memorial was one of the organizers of this conference, they and others had distanced themselves from the new political party "Democratic Union," which was challenging the Communist Party. As a matter of policy Memorial tried, from the outset, to foster a spirit of mutual cooperation with state officials, but not at the cost of principles.

Memorial's campaign, though often blocked, steadily gained ground. Support for Memorial as an organization or adherence to its principles was spreading. By June 1988, *Ogonyok* triumphantly reported that more than 10,000 signatures, including those of more than a hundred well-known writers, academicians, artists and public figures, were received by the USSR Supreme Soviet. The petition demanded the creation of both a monument and memorial center to the victims of the Stalinist purges. In the Chita region, east of Lake Baikal in Siberia, according to *Moscow News* KGB officers were even helping relatives of victims gain access to archives on Stalin's repressions. Alexei Solovyov, the KGB deputy director of the region, estimated that 11,332 people had been arrested and/or disappeared in this area between 1934 and 1939.[15] Since many documents had been falsified, he acknowledged, personal interviews were necessary to piece together the whole story. Some KGB officers from this region even appeared on television phone-in shows where the topic was mass repression and the goal was fund-raising for a plaque to Stalin's victims. A Chita bank account number was published in the newspaper soliciting donations for the fund, a first in the country.[16] Though this was viewed by many as merely a KGB image-polishing campaign, it could still be seen as a measure of acceptance. Especially in the Soviet Union, officials have to be very careful about the company they keep. In Leningrad, there was a late-night television broadcast of a meeting of thousands of citizens who had submitted a resolution to the 19th Party Conference demanding not only monuments to Stalin's victims all over the country but also a trial of Stalin.[17]

The 19th Party Conference of June 1988, which gathered 5,000 Communist Party members, was a welcome opportunity for Memorial to get official approval for a memorial in Moscow, but first the ground had to be prepared. Although Gorbachev had criticized Stalin's "enormous and unforgivable" crimes, and now scholars and writers were able to publish critical comments on Stalin, and although prominent Bolsheviks were rehabilitated, Memorial still felt that the process had to move farther and faster. Hundreds of supporters gathered around the monument in Pushkin Square demanding evidence of the repudiation of Stalin's Terror in the form of a monument to his victims. By this time, campaigns in thirty cities across the country (Riga, Chita, Kharkov, etc.) had gathered 30,000 signatures on their petitions.[18] At a news conference prior to the Party Conference in Moscow sponsored by the Novosti Press Agency (notorious among experts for its KGB connections), Yuri Samodurov outlined Memorial's idea for a monument complex with a library, archives and museum in Moscow. He explained that "the memorial will immortalize people's grief and memory about millions of compatriots who had been subjected to groundless repressions and would exonerate them politically."[19] Samodurov said that the signatories of his petition included *Novyi Mir* editor Sergei Zalyugin and *Ogonyok* magazine editor Vitaly Korotich. Samodurov referred to Khrushchev's de-Stalinization and explained that the current campaign focused on Stalinism more than Stalin.[20] Chita, Riga, Orel and Irkutsk had either planned or already built memorials, he reported. He also expressed the hope that after the conference a bank account would be opened to which private citizens and worker's collectives could send their contributions

The next pre-conference rally would hear calls for the notorious Lubyanka (central office of the KGB) to be used for the memorial, according to Yuri Skubko, a founding member of Memorial. Skubko was also one of the co-founders of the pro-Gorbachev "Perestroika Club."[21] Regarding the memorial, Skubko emphasized that a "permanent research center should record every name, every fate."[22] The June 25 rally of about three hundred people outside Dynamo stadium received official approval. Significantly, this occasion marked the first time that Andrei Sakharov took part in a street protest since the 1970s when he and his wife, Yelena Bonner, campaigned for the freedom of dissidents then being tried.[23] Sakharov's moral weight strengthened the developing organization. He spoke of how the monument fit into Gorbachev's restructuring program: "perestroika is our last chance to be a great country . . . perestroika must be pure, it must be for all people."[24] Other speakers included historian Yuri Afanasyev; writer Ales Adamovich; former political prisoners Larisa Bogoraz, Sergei Kovalyov and Lev Timofeyev; chairman of the Cinematographer's Union Yelem Klimov; and relatives of prominent

Bolsheviks, like Karl Radek's granddaughter, who had been Stalin's victims. While police just stood by at Memorial's rally, on that same day in another place in Moscow they broke up a rally of the Democratic Union, which was campaigning for a multi-party system and the abolition of political police.[25] This latter group was formed in response to police interference with a demonstration for de-Stalinization in March. At that time, some members of Memorial and other groups expressed the need for a legal opposition party. Memorial's more modest professed goals won them more official tolerance in this round.

Though the 19th Conference approved the memorial on July 1, this decision was perceived by many in Memorial as a bittersweet success. Since they considered the ideas as having come from the people, they resented the Party's appropriation of the idea as its own. After enduring harassment, arrests and threats from the government along the way to winning support for the idea, they felt it was the height of cynicism for the government to now take credit for what it had strenuously opposed. There was a fear that the memorial would be one more victim to state propaganda. Mikhail Kovalenko, an attorney and member of Memorial's initiative group, commented, "The state conducted the repressions, the state should not be the one to put up the memorial. They should give their approval, set up a community commission, and let them (the commission) collect the means to build it."[26]

On July 27, 1988, the Writer's Union weekly *Literaturnaya Gazeta* opened an account at the "USSR Social Bank" to collect donations for a monument.[27] This event marked the beginning of what might be termed a "sparring match" between Memorial and the Party. Decisions regarding the nature of the monument and control of the bank account were to become contested issues between the government and Memorial. The government tried to control both.

By mid-July, Memorial was putting its ideas into action. In an article entitled "Memorial of the Conscience," the popular weekly *Ogonyok* suggested an exhibition of projects for the monument to Stalin's victims in October and November at the Dom Kultury (Palace of Culture). It provided an address to which proposals could be sent.[28] A few issues later, the magazine reported a tremendous response—phone calls, inquiries, visits. *Ogonyok* stressed the point that people could send anything—ideas, concepts, amateur drawings. It urged people to be creative and exercise their "sacred right to remembrance." In this issue (No. 32, August 6–13, 1988), the magazine announced that at the last stage of the competition *Ogonyok* and Dom Kultury would conduct a "Week of Conscience," the proceeds of which would go to the Memorial fund. The event would

include expositions of historical materials, photographs, paintings, drawings, graphics, performances and films exposing the cult of personality; a
day of "repressed poetry" and "camp songs"; and an evening of remembrance "of people whose names were torn out of history in order to please
henchmen."[29] *Ogonyok* emphasized the idea that a single "leader" would
not be the focal point, that "Stalinism is worse than Stalin."[30] They would
instead discuss the sources and mechanisms of all cults as well as ways of
eradicating them in order to ensure democracy.

This article also touched on the social and psychological problems
connected with eradicating Stalin and totalitarianism from a totalitarian
system. The psychological aspects of Stalinism, combined with the "fear
and blood of millions have penetrated the conscience and the flesh in an
almost genetic way."[31] The goal of the Week of Conscience was to perform
a "cleansing" function, using genuine documents to establish what actually
took place. The article also dealt with the issue of segregating hangmen
from their victims, asserting that they cannot stay together in one party
and wondering aloud if the hangmen should be posthumously excluded
from the Party.

By August 25, 1988, significantly, Tass, the official news service,
announced that Memorial had held its constituent meeting in Moscow. It
quoted Vyacheslav Glazychev of the organizing committee and secretary
of the board of the USSR Architects Union as saying that Memorial's
objectives were the same as those of the CPSU Politburo commission
studying the repressions of the 1930s–1950s. The Architects Union would
cooperate in pursuing these, he explained, by collecting letters, reminiscences and photo materials from private citizens. The meeting, attended
by two hundred people, took place at the Architects Union headquarters.
The group gathered to discuss a number of issues, including the kind of
monument they wanted. Sukhanovka, a former monastery converted to a
prison under Stalin, was one suggestion for the location of the memorial.
Another important question raised was the determination of the number
of victims to be memorialized.[32] To this very day, efforts are being made
to ascertain a figure. This is certainly a task appropriate for the research
center. Among those present were Andrei Sakharov; Sergei Grigoryants,
the publisher of the unsanctioned journal *Glasnost*; the writers Anatoly
Rybakov and Mikhail Shatrov, who have addressed the horrors of Stalinism in their works; the Film and Architects Unions; and *Ogonyok* and
Literaturnaya Gazeta. Members elected to the advisory board for Memorial—which, as one article commented, "reads like a 'Who's who' of
reform in the Soviet Union"[33]—were chosen by readers of *Literaturnaya
Gazeta*, *Ogonyok* and opinion polls. They included Andrei Sakharov,

Yevgeny Yevtushenko, director of the Soviet Cultural Foundation, Dmitry Likhachev, the poet-singer Bulat Okudzhava, Boris Yeltsin, Yuri Afanasyev, Roy Medvedev, Anatoly Rybakov, Vasily Bykov, Mikhail Shatrov, Vitaly Korotich, Ales Adamovich, Georgy Baklanov, and Yuri Karyakin.[34] Finally, on the basis of a popular opinion survey, a telegram was sent to Alexander Solzhenitsyn in Vermont, asking if he would join the Council.[35] At this time a call was made for the restitution of Solzhenitsyn's citizenship and the publication of his banned works. Author Anatoly Rybakov made a speech at this conference, the closing lines of which eloquently define part of Memorial's function: "Memorial is a monument of grief for the millions of squandered lives and at the same time a monument to the triumph of justice. Memorial is a reminder and a warning."[36] Natalya Rappoport, a scientist whose father was one of the accused physicians in the Doctors Plot, made a speech in which she cited the death in prison of Anatoly Marchenko in 1986 as a modern-day repression.

Two weeks after the conference Memorial received a telegram from Alexander Solzhenitsyn, declining to participate in the advisory council. Expressing his gratitude for the invitation, Solzhenitsyn, who spent eight years in labor camps under Stalin and who was expelled from the Soviet Union after *Gulag Archipelago* was published in the West, explained:

To the memory of those who perished in 1918–1956, I have dedicated *Gulag Archipelago* for which I was rewarded with the accusation of treason. It is not possible to pass over this. Moreover, since I am located outside the country, there is no possibility of actually participating in its civic life.[37]

It should be noted that Solzhenitsyn's work includes the Lenin period as well.

In September 1988, a year after Memorial's emergence, some of its members began venturing to address such taboo subjects as Lenin's role in the repression. This historical society was increasingly resembling a political movement. Indeed, with such a clear set of anti-hegemonic values, it was ineluctably being drawn from learning the errors of history to applying its lessons, that is, politics. A pertinent article in *Russkaya Mysl* was based on Yuri Skubko's comments at the August 25 conference.[38] It recounted how resistance from conservative forces of the nomenklatura had not prevented an overwhelming majority of the population from supporting the memorial concept, thus giving Memorial both unofficial and official backing. Furthermore, the efforts of progressive publishers have done a great deal to promote the cleansing process, for example, by

preparing Vasily Grossman's novel, *Everything is Flowing*, for publication
(in installments in *Novyi Mir* in 1989). The novel's special significance
lies in the fact that it exposes Lenin's role in the creation of the totalitarian
state. Additionally, materials on the Brezhnev period (the trial of
Sinyavsky and Daniel) were beginning to be published.

The radical faction of Memorial, however, had even greater demands
than mainstream Memorial members and started expressing them. They
asserted that the KGB headquarters at the Lubyanka would be a fitting
place for the memorial. They also wanted to expand Memorial's time
frame to include the period from 1917 to the present in order to create a
tribute to all victims of the totalitarian regime. This would include such
victims as Gumilyov and the St. Petersburg workers (shot in January 1918)
as well as Vasily Stus and Anatoly Marchenko. Skubko, Kovalenko and
others argued that in order for Memorial to make progress it must promote
different ideas than it had the previous year.[39] Thus, they asserted, all
historical truth without deletion must be uncovered, and a memorial to the
victims of totalitarianism must be created. A government that is unaccount-
able and that is maintained by a "system of fear" must be totally over-
hauled. The changes could start with the dissolution of the dreaded KGB
but still allow the possibility of some other type of democratic security
services. Furthermore, Skubko continued, the exposé should include the
KGB stool pigeons as well as a broader publication of KGB archives
(starting with those of the Cheka). Finally, this commentary pointed out
that the informing purpose of the memorial could not be realized while
there still existed prisoners of conscience, political articles of the criminal
code, punitive psychiatry and the banishment of the author of the *Gulag
Archipelago*.

Though Memorial tried to keep a low profile, its unwillingness to give
up on its core principles made its members vulnerable at all times to official
harassment. Dmitry Yurasov, a history student and member of Memorial,
was detained on September 16, 1988, by the KGB at the Dnepropetrovsk
airport before returning to Moscow. He had visited the city to give a speech
entitled "A Chronicle of Stalin's Crimes." The KGB wanted to know who
had organized Yurasov's trip and lecture and what his connections were
with the Democratic Union.[40]

After its constituent meeting, Memorial sought to establish a fitting date
for the "Day of Sorrowful Remembrance." Following its usual procedure,
Memorial turned for guidance to a survey of public opinion. Among its
sources were letters from readers of *Literaturnaya Gazeta*. Some suggested the "deep, gloomy fall of November"; others named February 25,

the anniversary of Khrushchev's Secret Speech; others proposed the May 18 anniversary of the Shakhty trial, termed "the first large-scale act of state political terrorism in (our) country."[41] The date of Stalin's death, March 5, and the final trial dates of Bukharin, Tukhachevsky and Yakir were also suggested. There was, however, one date that received the most recognition—December 1. That was the day Sergei Kirov was murdered; the day that ushered in the Great Terror, the dread period when all who were perceived as "enemies of the people" were eliminated.

Of course, different people have different reasons for being involved with Memorial. In an interview in *Uchitelskaya Gazeta*, Yakov Etinger, a member of the executive committee of Memorial's Social Council, described his reasons. After reading an article in *Literaturnaya Gazeta* on Memorial's goals, he decided to contribute his own reminiscences of those times. His father, a well-known doctor and professor, was arrested in November 1950. The charges included the following: a statement he made to the effect that if Lenin were still alive, everything would be different; "cosmopolitanism"; public criticism of Lysenko; and "criminal (medical) treatment of a Politburo member." This was considered the first link to the Doctors Plot. Yakov Etinger and his mother were also arrested under Article 58 (anti-Soviet propaganda). They were eventually rehabilitated. Etinger described how many people like himself spent their youthful years imprisoned and how it is therefore symbolically appropriate that the youth are taking the most active part in the work of Memorial.[42]

During this period, the 3 x 4 meter office given to Memorial by the Cinematographers Union had already received thousands of letters, and people were lining up daily to tell their tales of repression. The room was no longer large enough to accommodate the numbers of people who came there and the volume of records accumulating. Therefore, the Social Council sent a letter to the chairman of the executive committee of the Moscow City Council, V. T. Saikin, with the request to register the organizational committee of Memorial and to allot a space of 200 square meters in order to be able to preserve personal accounts, diaries, copies of documents and other articles from camp and prison life.[43] Etinger stressed the importance of speeding up the process while eyewitnesses were still alive. He also mentioned that the Architects Union was discussing the possibility of turning the former Sukhanovka prison into a museum and archive. This was reported in an article entitled "The Living Need It."[44] Memorial was able to utilize many such articles to inform the public about their organization, gather more documentation and broaden their base of support.

The Moscow Memorial is a prototype and major local division of the All-Union (now Interrepublic) Memorial in both form and function. Similar activities were taking place in other parts of the country. By early October 1988, for example, the Chita bank account to the victims of repression from the 1930s to the 1950s had collected around 30,000 rubles and some hard currency.[45] In Leningrad, before its chapter of Memorial was registered, the group used the office of the Soviet Cultural Foundation as a base and meeting place. In consequence the Foundation, together with the college of lawyers, became one of the founders of the Leningrad Memorial. The leadership met there and funds that people sent for the monument went into the account of the Leningrad Cultural Foundation. Its chairman, Dmitry Likhachev (member of the Social Council), was himself a political prisoner and, according to Tatyana Pritykina, believed very strongly in the importance of the historical, cultural and moral education of people.[46] Tatyana Pritykina was also a founding member of the Leningrad Memorial. This division of Memorial organizes an evening of remembrance with various related themes every Monday night at the House of Culture. When entrance fees are charged, they go into the monument account. In the coming pages, we will take a closer look at the Leningrad (now St. Petersburg) and other Memorial divisions.

With the revelations publicized by Memorial, there followed a wave of anger and agitation for revenge. The newspaper *Semya* described a mass grave near the Donskoy crematorium marked by a white stone with the words, "Communal grave number one," where many victims were dumped after a "conveyer-belt" execution. *Semya* called for the prosecutor and KGB to investigate exactly where the remains were dispersed.[47] In the Kuropaty forest, more mass graves were found in which an estimated 102,000 victims were buried. Facts like these and others have led many to compare the Stalin era with the Nazi Third Reich.[48] Gradually Medvedev's and Solzhenitsyn's writings were being printed in the Soviet Union, as were Nadezhda Mandelshtam's and Evgeniya Ginzburg's memoirs of the Stalin era, fueling anti-Stalinist emotion. A radical wing of Memorial felt that it was fitting to organize a trial of Stalin in the famous House of Columns where Bukharin and many other revolutionaries had been sentenced to death in "show trials." With this "anti-show trial," Memorial envisaged something between the international Russell Tribunal, which investigated American complicity in Vietnam, and the 1946 Nuremburg Trials of Nazi war criminals.

Memorial, however, faces a considerable amount of opposition from neo-Stalinists. For example, Ivan Shekhovtsev, a retired Ukrainian, had gone to court seventeen times to defend the "honor and dignity" of Stalin!

He had also tried to sue Ales Adamovich for referring to Stalin's interrogators as "henchmen."[49] Shekhovtsev presented the argument that innocence must be presumed, because it could not be proved that illegal methods like torture were used. He lost the case. Since what was being challenged was not just a pernicious person but a pernicious system that was still in power, the probability of a trial at that time was very slight.

Memorial held its first conference in the theater of the Cinematographers Union on the last weekend of October 1988. In a speech on the first day, Andrei Sakharov urged the organization not to limit its efforts to condemning Stalin's crimes but to look also at the crimes committed under Khrushchev and Brezhnev, and to aid in the rehabilitation of the victims of these repressions.[50] He also called for the release of all political prisoners. On the second day of the two-day conference, which was attended by around six hundred delegates from all over the Soviet Union, Sakharov was proposed as a candidate for the Soviet parliament (the People's Deputies would be chosen in April 1989). A change in the electoral law the previous week had allowed groups like Memorial to elect some candidates. There were further calls for a political organization to prevent the resurgence of political oppression. In a later interview with Radio Liberty, former Soviet dissident Vladimir Tolts pointed out that in promoting Sakharov as a candidate for the Congress of People's Deputies, Memorial had decided to achieve its political goals by completely political means.[51]

By the time of the first conference, the Moscow division of Memorial had gained official approval, but other cities, like Minsk, complained at the conference of continuing harassment by local authorities. A rally of the Minsk Memorial was broken up by the police with water cannons and people were arrested. Memorial resolved to send a telex to the Kremlin, protesting police tactics in Minsk. Looking to the Kremlin for support was certainly a unique phenomenon for a reform group, and a measure of their growing stature.

This conference highlighted many of the issues with which Memorial had grappled from the very beginning: How far should Memorial go in its examination of the repressions? Should it concentrate exclusively on Stalin's victims or include political prisoners of earlier and later periods as well? Should it try to reform the political system through historical enlightenment activities or through political activism? Finally, how rapidly should this be pursued? Two significant answers to these questions were to be found in the unanimous agreement on the nomination of Andrei Sakharov for the Soviet parliament and on the call for restoration of

Solzhenitsyn's Soviet citizenship. Their individual contributions to freedom of the repressed and the symbolic importance of each encompassed nearly all of the issues.

The political activism that Memorial and others were promoting compelled officials to address the subject of political prisoners. On November 1, 1988, Soviet Justice Minister Boris Kravtsov asserted that there were only ten known political prisoners—five incarcerated under laws banning anti-Soviet and religious activity and five in internal exile. Western estimates were around two hundred. Some of this discrepancy was due to respective definitions of the term "political prisoner." The figure of two hundred included those incarcerated under falsified charges or held in psychiatric institutions for political reasons.[52] Regardless of whether or not Memorial decided to expand its aims to include later political prisoners, the very fact that the issue was under discussion made it difficult for anyone to ignore.

In early November 1988, the first meeting of former Moscow prisoners of Stalin's camps took place in the city's Central House of Artists. It was resolved that a close cooperation with Memorial would be crucial to both. Nikolai Starkov wrote in *Moskovskiye Novosti*: "Our goal is not only to construct a monument to those who died, but also to remember the living, help them. There are less of them with every passing day. They cannot wait."[53]

In the meantime, support for Memorial was also coming from outside the Soviet Union. In London, in mid-November 1988, actress Vanessa Redgrave and British film director Sir Richard Attenborough organized a concert featuring the work of Soviet musicians, poets, playwrights and artists. It was a remembrance of the cultural works that were repressed under Stalin. The proceeds from this concert went to Memorial.[54]

At the same time, a concert featuring Okudzhava, Pozhenyan, and Zakharov as well as artists of the Taganka and Sovremennik theaters was being given in Moscow. It was sponsored by the journals *Teatr*, *Iskusstvo Kino*, *Sovetsky Ekran*, by the union Soyuzteatr and the founders of Memorial.[55] The proceeds of this event would also go toward the creation of a monument to the victims of Stalinist repressions. The concert was not advertised in newspapers or on posters. Notice was spread simply by word of mouth. An article entitled "Be Silent as the Curtain in Front of the Terror Rises"[56] addressed the issue of how difficult it is to talk about Stalin's crimes in a land where people learned on pain of death to be silent rather than speak about the past. Many in the audience were the sons and daughters of victims who, in turn, brought along their own children.[57] This new generation is of vital importance to Memorial in its efforts to foster a new consciousness as well as a conscience, which for so many decades was stifled in the Soviet Union.

By November 15, 1988, as preparations for the "Week of Conscience" at the MELZ (Moscow Electric Light Bulb Factory) Palace of Culture were under way, *Ogonyok* and the Palace of Culture announced in a press release that they had already received a total of 1,460 packages, letters and projects for the monument. These contained stories of illegal repressions, information on the fates of families, and various documents for the Wall of Remembrance. On this wall people attached personal effects, notes saying "who knew my father. . . ," photographs, newspaper articles, and announcements on rehabilitation.[58] The Week, which opened on November 19, 1988, was so arranged that a different organization (e.g., the Theater Union, Leningrad, *Ogonyok*, etc.) took part each day. On one day there were special services in Moscow churches. Another event was a service conducted by Father Gleb Yakunin, a dissident orthodox priest who had been exiled for ten years under Brezhnev, in Kalitnikov Cemetery, one of the mass burial sites for Stalin's victims.[59] There was a permanent exhibition of proposals for the memorial complex as well as an information center in which Dmitry Yurasov, the Historical Archive Institute student and Memorial activist, continued his collection work on victims. He had already identified the names of 134,000 victims, many of whom had been sentenced to death. On one wall hung a map displaying black crosses to designate camps under Stalin. Contributions toward the monument were placed by visitors in a wheelbarrow with a blood-stained sign on it that read, "for the memorial to the victims of Stalin's repressions."[60] Many five- and ten-ruble notes (a significant amount at the time) were donated, sometimes with the names of murdered family members written on them. Over 50,000 rubles were collected.[61]

The program generally received a warm welcome, but the voices of Stalin's defenders could still be heard. Some visitors criticized the anti-Stalinist theme of the exhibit, saying that everyone was guilty of wrongdoing, not just one man.[62] Prior to the opening of the event, *Moskovsky Komsomolets* printed a letter from a retired engineer who lamented that the funds collected during the week would go toward a memorial "to enemies of the people and criminals." It continued, "no honest person feared arrest. Only those who were mixed up in something. And some deliberately sought to get into prison to avoid being sent to the front in the looming war."[63]

Fortunately for Memorial, other letters supported its position. On the first day of the Week of Conscience, an article appeared in the Soviet Trade Union daily *Trud* announcing that the Stalin museum in his birthplace of

Gori, Georgia, was officially closed (it had unofficially closed in September). According to the Ministry of Culture, it would be reopened and would show objective documents on Stalin and Stalinism "as a warning against any resurrection of his cult."[64] Stalinism was finally being officially exposed, but Memorial had a long way to go.

NOTES

Because there is to date no historiographical literature on Memorial, the source material for this section is derived from newspaper and journal articles (from the Western and Soviet press), press releases, reports and personal interviews.

1. This chronicle of events from August to December 1987 is derived from *Russkaya Mysl* (Moscow), 5 February 1988.

2. Joshua Rubenstein, *Soviet Dissidents: Their Struggle for Human Rights* (Boston: Beacon Press, 1980), p. 37.

3. *Russkaya Mysl.*
4. Ibid.
5. Ibid.
6. Ibid.
7. Ibid.
8. Ibid.
9. Ibid.
10. *UPI*, 7 March 1988.
11. Ibid.
12. Ibid.
13. Ibid.
14. *Chicago Tribune*, 9 May 1988.
15. *Reuters*, 16 June 1988.
16. Ibid.
17. *Tanjug* (Yugoslavia), 17 June 1988.
18. *AP*, 18 June 1988.
19. *UPI*, 22 June 1988.
20. Ibid.
21. *Guardian* (London), 27 June 1988.
22. Ibid., 23 June 1988.
23. *AP*, 25 June 1988.
24. *Reuters*, 25 June 1988.
25. Ibid.
26. *New York Times*, 3 July 1988.
27. *Tass*, 27 July 1988.
28. *Ogonyok* 29, 14–21 July 1988.
29. Ibid., 32, 6–13 August 1988.
30. Ibid.

31. Ibid.

32. *AP*, 26 August 1988.

33. *Reuters*, 31 August 1988.

34. *Agence France Presse*, 26 August 1988.

35. *Daily Frankfurter Rundschau*, 27 August 1988.

36. *Literaturnaya Gazeta* 35, September 1988.

37. *New York Times*, 8 September 1988.

38. *Russkaya Mysl*, 23 September 1988.

39. Ibid.

40. *Times* (London), 10 October 1988.

41. *Literaturnaya Gazeta*, 28 September 1988.

42. *Uchitelskaya Gazeta*, 6 October 1988.

43. *Vechernyaya Moskva*, 20 October 1988.

44. Ibid.

45. *Komsomolskaya Pravda*, 6 October 1988.

46. Tatyana Pritykina, interview held at the Leningrad Cultural Foundation, Leningrad, April 16, 1990.

47. *Sunday Times* (London), 16 October 1988.

48. *Washington Post*, 23 October 1988.

49. *Sunday Times* (London), 16 October 1988.

50. *Reuters*, 30 October 1988.

51. Radio Liberty, "Sakharov and Memorial," 31 October 1988.

52. *Baltimore Sun*, 1 November 1988.

53. *Moskovskiye Novosti*, 6 November 1988.

54. *AP*, 11 November 1988.

55. *Literaturnaya Gazeta*, 9 November 1988.

56. *Die Welt*, 17 November 1988.

57. Ibid.

58. *Znaniye Sila*, January 1988.

59. *Financial Times* (London), 21 November 1988.

60. *AP*, 19 November 1988.

61. *New York Times*, 28 December 1988.

62. Ibid.

63. *Reuters*, 19 November 1988.

64. Ibid.

CHAPTER 5 _____

1988–1989: Toward the Founding Conference

In a December 1988 article in *Nedelya*, Suzanna Alperina, a Moscow University student, contended that Memorial's Organizational Committee workspace was too small to do an adequate job and that this limitation might be worse than nothing. The insufficient space allotted Memorial at Chernyakovsky 2 sent a clear message to the country. Alperina used a Russian expression to describe how in the stuffy room, always packed with visitors, there was "not even space for an apple." She added that by November 24, 1988, there were already 1,640 names of callers and visitors in the log and new documents as well as donations poured in daily. The *Great Soviet Encyclopedia*, edited by Nikolai Bukharin, was one of many donations. So there remained little choice but to keep a great many of the archives in people's homes. Such circumstances led an elderly visitor to remark, "I probably will not see this memorial. And if such an attitude toward the organizational committee of Memorial is maintained, then, I am afraid that even my grandchild will not see it."[1]

Though Memorial was not receiving the official recognition it deserved, it was gaining widespread popularity in unofficial circles. On December 6, 1988, the founding meeting of the Ukrainian Memorial took place in the Kiev Movie House. It was described as a society for the preservation of the memory of victims of Stalinism and the liquidation of the consequences of Stalinshchina (Stalin's reign of terror). Les Tanyuk, who was named chairman, is a theater director and has been a participant in the Ukrainian democratic movement since the 1960s. He was exiled from Ukraine for two decades. Tanyuk had hoped to turn the "Kiev Youth

Theater" into the "Ukrainian National Theater," carrying on the tradition of Les Kurbas, who was "destroyed by Stalinist cutthroats."[2] He also conducted cultural evenings at the theater. During one of these he called for the publication of poems by the Ukrainian poet Vasily Stus, who died in a Perm camp in 1985. Not only was this proposal rejected by the Ukrainian authorities, but Tanyuk was dismissed from his job as director of the Kiev Youth Theater. Of considerable comfort to him was the fact that he could still rely on Memorial's support.[3]

Since July 1988, Memorial had been permitted to follow its course relatively unhindered, enjoying semi-official approval, at least with regard to the monument. But December brought with it unexpected bureaucratic obstacles. An article in *Sovetskaya Kultura* on December 27, 1988, announced the opening of a competition sponsored by the Ministry of Culture and others (including the leadership of the Artists and Architects Unions, who were also co-founders of Memorial) for a design for a monument to victims of lawlessness and repression in the years of the cult of personality. The memorial would be built in Moscow only. The competition was to be carried out in two stages—the first, to choose a place and concept for it; the second, to select a detailed plan. Memorial, whose thousands of signatures to the June Party Conference compelled the Party to approve the creation of a memorial to Stalin's victims, was not even mentioned in the article.[4] Additionally, Memorial's Founding Conference, it should be recalled, was supposed to have been held on December 17 and 18. The authorities, however, managed to block the original date by citing a technical requirement that the movement's constitution be published one month before the Founding Conference. Vitaly Korotich, editor of *Ogonyok*, vowed that he would publish it if no one else did by January 10.

The appropriation of the memorial project as its own was not the only way in which the Ministry of Culture undermined Memorial. It also rejected Memorial's proposal for a memorial complex and monuments in other cities by decreeing that only one monument would be built and that one would be in Moscow. This action can be seen as evidence that Memorial, which already had supporters in 110 cities, was becoming a threat to the authorities, many of whom felt that the continued revelations of Stalin's crimes was damaging their prestige and encouraging insubordination.[5] The authorities were fearful that Memorial might develop into an independent political movement like the popular fronts in the Baltic republics. To forestall this possibility, Memorial was not allocated the guaranteed number of seats in the new parliament. According to one article, only groups "of proven reliability" received these.[6] One-third of the 2,250 places were reserved for public organizations, but because of the state-engineered delay in the Founding Conference, Memorial could not make the January 26 deadline for nominating candidates. Memorial had to turn to its contacts in creative unions and government institutions to endorse Sakharov and other Memorial figures for the March 26 elections. The honorary chairman of Memorial, Andrei Sakharov, did not initially receive the needed endorsement from the Academy of Sciences; but due in large part to Memorial's rallying efforts, Sakharov eventually received the needed endorsement, first from the Institute of World Economy and then from the Academy of Sciences.[7]

Memorial called a news conference in response to the Ministry of Culture's announcement of the monument competition. Memorial felt betrayed, because, as they said, they had consistently sought cooperation, not confrontation, with the authorities and public organizations.[8] Just prior to this, the poet Yevgeny Yevtushenko, one of Memorial's activists, had called the Minister of Culture, Vasily Zakharov, to try to work out their differences, but it was to no avail. Yevtushenko asserted, "I think this is an effort to shake off the historical memory with the help of one or another stone or bronze monument. . . . This appears to be a blow against our organization as a whole."[9] On January 3, an interview with the Minister of Culture was published. Although it did not make reference to Memorial, it did mention using the monument's bank account, which already contained 1.5 million rubles. As long as Memorial was not a juridical entity (i.e., not registered), Memorial could not withdraw anything from this account. Writer Yuri Karyakin called it an "extraordinarily dangerous symptom of continued government monopoly over social activity despite President Mikhail S. Gorbachev's reforms."[10] Similar views were shared by Yuri Afanasyev and Vitaly Korotich. Afanasyev emphasized the need for the Soviet people to know their past and be aware of it: "We must create the antithesis of Stalinism . . . we must put the Stalinist era on trial so that people can understand it" as a means of purging the country's guilty conscience.[11] Ales Adamovich, a Byelorussian writer, described the official resistance to his republic's chapter of Memorial following the discovery of a mass grave containing 150,000 victims at Kuropaty near Minsk. The official press in Minsk had been conducting a campaign to discredit Memorial organizers, and Adamovich feared this would be a signal to local authorities to continue their opposition.[12]

During this time, many other Memorial-related issues were being debated. The actual number of victims, for example, was and is a very important question for Memorial. In an article in *Moscow News*, Roy Medvedev, a dissident Marxist historian and member of Memorial, estimated that as many as eight million people may have died during the famine and collectivization campaign before it; five to seven million people were victims of the purges; one million died during deportations of nations suspected of German collaboration; another five million people were sent to camps after the war.[13] As new material becomes available, the statistics are regularly revised. Medvedev was one of the early and few outspoken opponents of Stalinism to survive, but he is now joined by many. Anatoly Rybakov noted the growing danger of people "rushing to criticize Stalin, even those who previously used to glorify him," because it could become just another "meaningless political ritual."[14] This is one of the reasons why Memorial does not want to allow Stalin's repressions to be written off with just a single monument in Moscow.

On January 15, 1989, the Moscow section of Memorial held its founding conference. This chapter alone had 500 members, from which sixty were selected to be representatives at the forthcoming All-Union Founding Conference.[15] The Moscow Memorial adopted a charter (in May of 1989) that was more or less the same as that of the All-Union Society except that it did not allow collective membership.

A week later, on January 22, 1989, a meeting was held at the House of Cinematographers to promote Sakharov for People's Deputy. Oleg Orlov, a former candidate in biology who gave up his studies to concentrate on Memorial, introduced Sakharov to the gathering and lauded the human rights defender's activism. Ales Adamovich and poet Sylvia Kaputikyan also gave supportive speeches at the meeting. Thereafter, Sakharov presented his platform to resounding applause. He was unanimously confirmed by Memorial as a candidate for Moscow Region No. 1. Academicians Sagdeyev and Likhachev of the Soviet Cultural Foundation were also promoted and confirmed.[16] By organizing support for these candidates, Memorial's political voice became more and more audible.

In response to official unwillingness to provide a conference site for the unregistered organization, Memorial threatened to hold the congress in apartments. That proved unnecessary. The All-Union Society Memorial triumphantly held its Founding Conference at the Moscow Aviation Institute's House of Culture on January 28 and 29, 1989. The event attracted a large group—over five hundred delegates as well as hundreds of guests from more than one hundred cities. Many well-known figures in the scientific, cultural and art worlds attended. A number of delegates from Alma-Ata, Kiev and other cities reported that they were threatened by local authorities for trying to attend the Founding Conference, but they nevertheless managed to get there. Though Memorial did not enjoy official status, its activities were well publicized by reporters from the Soviet press, radio and television. In addition, foreign journalists were present for the event. Besides confirming a charter, resolutions, and a common set of moral principles, the congress also elected a Social Council consisting of seventeen prominent figures, a Scientific Council, an administrative Board of two hundred people, and a work group of twenty to tend to operational matters.

The conference opened with a moment of silent remembrance of the victims of Stalinism. Some had only to remember their own plight. When Afanasyev asked all the "victims of Stalin in the room to stand," old men and women slowly rose from their seats, as one journalist commented, "like ghosts."[17] During the deliberations, members of the Social Council and other attendees were allowed to express themselves freely. Some speakers labeled the killings of millions of Soviet citizens in the 1930s and 1940s "a crime against humanity."[18] Ales Adamovich pointed out that these representatives of 108 cities had:

different languages, different cultures, different nations. That is what separates people now in our society. But Memorial is what brings us closer. Memorial unites people in their feeling of aversion toward henchmen and their deeds, in their feeling of compassion and guilt toward victims. This . . . bringing different people together . . . is a very important concept for Memorial.[19]

In a more strident note, Adamovich called for Nuremberg-type trials against Stalin and his men and restitution to victims of Stalinism from the Soviet state similar to that granted Jews by the German state.[20] Invoking poetic justice, he said, "We should have as many pillars erected to this plague as there were statues of Stalin."[21]

In a chaotic time, with society in the throes of restructuring, Memorial found a common goal around which to rally. It also institutionalized that goal with an effective and growing organization. It is not surprising that this made the state apprehensive.

Andrei Sakharov asserted that millions of Soviet citizens were lost to illegal repression, organized famine, lawlessness and terror; that:

Only a social organization like Memorial can reach these individual human fates, in any case can try to do this. No official organization, constrained by political or any kind of caste considerations can do this. It is only in our power . . . as a social, democratic organization.[22]

In other words, considering Soviet history, politics is too important to reside exclusively in the hands of the present politicians.

Yevtushenko warned of the dangers to the press and to writers if glasnost is undermined. He argued:

if we cannot rescue anyone or anything from the past, we at least can rescue the present from repetition of the tragic crimes and the mistakes which have brought our country to the brink of spiritual and economic catastrophe.[23]

Korotich emphasized the importance of gathering documentary evidence to put Stalinism on trial, but asserted that "the trial must be based on archives rather than emotions."[24] Korotich cautioned that "the teeth of the dragon, the black teeth of Stalinism were still able to sting."[25] He explained that out of every eight letters received by *Ogonyok*, one curses their cause, threatening, "we'll return yet!"[26]

Poet A. A. Voznesensky addressed the momentous issue of what could be the most fitting way to commemorate "30 million victims, 30 million ghosts."[27] He argued that the best memorial would not be made of stone or copper but of complete democracy, the only bulwark against the emergence of a new Stalinism. He asserted that the national front that had formed to fight Stalinism had no analogy in history.

Baklanov, editor of the liberal journal *Znamya*, warned that the difficult economic situation of the country could provide the last hope for Stalinists and all those who are against perestroika.[28] All addressed the problem of the vulnerability of Soviet society to Stalinism during that time of change and reorganization, emphasizing the need to support glasnost and perestroika—indeed, to promote the irreversibility of these processes and to support the government's philosophy, implying a continuing suspicion of the government's actions.

A detailed examination of the Charter provides some interesting insights (see Appendix B for text of the complete Charter). The first section of the All-Union Society Memorial's Charter carries perhaps a larger message than that which is explicitly stated. First, the organization declares that its activities are in agreement with the constitution of the Soviet Union, the legislation of the Soviet Union and autonomous republics and with the international legal obligations of the Soviet Union.[29] Furthermore, it declares its disagreement with lawlessness and discrimination, support for recovering the rights of individuals and peoples, and condemnation of arbitrariness and force as a means of solving social problems and social conflicts. Memorial's insistence on allying itself with officially accepted principles permits it to challenge its official detractors as hypocritical. In addition, Memorial wanted to emphasize its legality and thereby dispel any negative image of itself as an underground opposition movement. In the structure of Memorial as outlined here,

the Society Memorial consists of local divisions and other forms of organization . . . acting on the principles of autonomy and self-government. . . . [A]
central electoral organ coordinates the activities of local societies and determines the Charter.

One might infer a role model, as it were, a prescription for the state. A later
point states that local societies are at liberty to decide on the form and
method of their activities as well as their internal structures. In essence it
is the state constitution writ small—with large implications for the state.

   Many of the goals and programmatic forms of Memorial's activities that
are spelled out in the second part of the Charter have already been
described. It is useful here to examine a few of the basic premises, such
as "the preservation and immortalization of the memory of victims of
Stalinism." One can argue that the use of the word "victim" implies
criminal perpetrators. Witness the following goal as stated by the Charter:

The creation of . . . a Memorial complex, including a monument to the victims
of Stalinism, and also a scientific-information and enlightenment center with a
publicly accessible archive, museum and library, materials that contain information on the repressions of Stalinism.

By stressing the significance of the information center, Memorial is
contending that there can be no lasting change without knowledge. Most
believe, however, that knowledge is not enough. Delegates to the conference later told *Ogonyok*, "we should work in such a way that even the air
around the monuments becomes different."[30] The last of Memorial's goals
urges:

active participation in democratic transformations, assistance in the development of a civic and legal consciousness in fellow citizens, struggle against illegal
acts, education of the younger generation in the spirit of a legal government.

The use of the words "active participation" implies approval of Memorial's
involvement in political activity. Memorial expressed the hope of fulfilling
the Charter's goals by influencing public consciousness and opinion
through "mass information, lectures, signature campaigns and other legal
methods."

   Throughout the Charter, Memorial emphasizes its twin roles as both
loyal opposition and microcosm of democracy. In the section on membership it specifies that "membership in the Society Memorial is incompatible
with propaganda or the practices of national or religious intolerance, and
anti-humanist ideas," and "members of the Society Memorial occupying

staff positions in the apparatus of the Society may not be elected to the central organs of the Society." This seems designed to prevent a conflict of interest that might compromise its role as an extra-official monitor of the state.

Another example of the democratic traditions embodied in the Charter can be seen in the system of checks and balances it institutes. For example, votes are conducted only when the required number of voters is present. Estimates made by the leadership on expenditures as well as the general work can be approved only by the Social Council, whose members have been chosen by polling the population.

Finally, the fiscal policy of the Memorial society and foundation are explained. Income derives from: voluntary contributions and donations; bequests and other payments of citizens, institutions, enterprises and organizations in the Soviet Union and abroad; from publishing, lectures, receipts from concerts and other events as well as introductory and membership dues. The financing of various programs must be agreed upon by the local societies involved, the leadership and the supporting foreign organizations (where applicable). Every point of the nine-page Charter was debated at length and voted on. It was adopted amidst applause with only one dissenting vote.

Based on the principles of the Charter, twenty-one resolutions were passed at the conference. They include requests for: the realization of the spirit and letter of the 19th Party Conference's decision and the Charter's goals; the release of arrested members of the committee "Karabakh" (Armenian activists promoting the Union of Nagorno-Karabakh with Armenia); the rehabilitation of political prisoners of the post-Stalin era; the restitution of Alexander Solzhenitsyn's Soviet citizenship and the publication of his *Gulag Archipelago* and other works. Significantly, the congress came out against the criminal prosecution of those still living who were responsible for carrying out Stalin's repressions. This was due, in large part, to the influence of Andrei Sakharov and Yelena Bonner who felt that Memorial should not play the role of prosecutor.[31] However, Memorial's congress did take the position that massive illegal repressions are crimes and that a public trial against Stalin should be conducted. These measures were directed toward moral purification. This did not mean, though, that the trial issue was resolved. The conference also appealed to the Supreme Soviet to remove Articles 70 and 190-1 from the RSFSR Criminal Code (anti-Soviet agitation and propaganda, circulating deliberately false fabrications defaming the Soviet political and social system). One of the resolutions confirmed support for Andrei Sakharov's platform. Another resolution expressed the hope for cooperation with commissions studying repression, reiterating an earlier statement made to the government commission established after the 70th anniversary of the revolution. The rapid publication of the entire stenographic record of Khrushchev's XX and XXII Congresses was also called for in this document. Finally, the conference confirmed the Scientific Council of the research center: A. M. Adamovich, Y. N. Afanasyev, M. Y. Gefter, N. N. Pokrovsky, V. D. Polikarpov, D. I. Raskin, M. O. Chudakova, Y. Y. Etinger, N. G. Okhotin and A. B. Roginsky.

The hall of the Aviation Institute was an example of what the future center might look like. A huge map of the Gulag Archipelago was displayed, marking sixty-nine corrective labor camps, twenty-one "special prisons" and five "transfer prisons" dispersed throughout the Soviet Union. An illustrated biography of Stalin complete with photographs of the self-glorifying statues he had erected could be found there. Biographical data on Stalin's rivals, Bukharin and Trotsky, were also provided in the exhibition.[32]

An eight-page newspaper with articles by Memorial was available at the conference. Not surprisingly, there is a story attached to these stories. The newspaper was almost banned on the eve of the gathering. Arseny Roginsky explained that the original contract with the printer was for 30,000 copies of the paper. It was to contain an appeal for the restitution of Solzhenitsyn's citizenship and an announcement of Sakharov's parliamentary nomination, in addition to articles by the group's leaders. The official government censor apparently disapproved of the proposal. The government said it would only allow 2,000 copies with no mention of Solzhenitsyn or Sakharov. In a phone conversation with a Central Committee official, Afanasyev threatened to cancel the paper and call the attention of the international press to the issue. Finally, 5,000 copies were agreed upon; the Sakharov announcement was kept, but the Solzhenitsyn announcement was excluded. In the lower left hand corner of the second page, in compliance with Memorial's demand, a space was left blank where the Solzhenitsyn appeal had been deleted. Roginsky explained, "That's our little message to the public."[33] Since, in the sphere of communication, "nothing never happens,"[34] it was a powerful message.

Indeed, the public was receiving a lot of Memorial's messages. After the Founding Conference, Memorial leaders elaborated on some of the society's ideas in the press. In an article in *Novoye Vremya*,[35] illustrated by a picture of the Gulag map as well as picture of a $100 check for the Memorial fund from an American supporter, Ales Adamovich addressed issues of the conference. He asserted that the work of Memorial today, in essence, already constituted a trial against Stalinism. Adamovich explained that in cities like Karaganda, Vorkuta and Magadan, people were collecting documents and openly publishing names of the henchmen and their victims. Some groups within Memorial find this a sufficient proceeding against Stalinism, that is, trial in the arena of public opinion without prosecution. They promote the view that punishing Stalinism with Stalinist methods is not the way to eliminate Stalinism.[36] Others disagree. This issue will be discussed further in the next chapters.

In an article in *Moscow News*, Yuri Afanasyev, Memorial's co-chairman, eloquently described the society as a political, cultural, legal and moral organization. He talked about how ridding Soviet society of the yoke of Stalinism also required giving up the idea of achieving a "false unanimity" in exchange for allowing the expression of varying views. Afanasyev asserted that Memorial's first task in building a civil society was to examine the past, since it lives on in the present. "Thus," he commented, "Memorial is a political movement. This will be the case until we settle accounts with the past."[37] The history that people need to learn is not only the politics of the past but the culture of the past as well. For this reason, he also labeled Memorial a cultural movement. Furthermore, when Afanasyev talked about Memorial's desire that law become an integral part of public consciousness, he called the society a legal movement. The co-chairman recounted tales of obstruction by authorities in the cities of Minsk, Alma-Ata, Saratov, Kiev, and Orel, among others. Despite confirming evidence, including witnesses' accounts of mass graves of thousands of Stalin's victims outside Bykovnya near Kiev, authorities would still not acknowledge these findings, claiming lack of documentation. Rallies to commemorate and rebury the dead were also forbidden in Orel, where political prisoners in Orel prison were shot in September 1941. Afanasyev concluded, "the forces of the past sense the rise of democracy and dread it. To them, Memorial means the inexorable progress of our society toward democratization."[38] The restructuring of social relations characteristically makes those in power uncomfortable.

Afanasyev alluded to, but did not elaborate on, internal difficulties within Memorial. He simply stated, "we should first and foremost be a moral movement, a movement of conscience."[39] This probably was a reference to internal power struggles and conflicts about issues such as how to deal with Stalin's surviving henchmen. Afanasyev mused about Orwell's state in which "He who controls the past controls the future, and he who controls the present, controls the past," contrasting it with Memorial's ideal that no single ideology would control anything.[40] Indeed, according to Afanasyev, Memorial wanted to develop a social conscience and promote appropriate feelings of guilt and repentance through knowledge and realization. He pointed out that in many languages conscience and consciousness share the same meaning. Memorial's formidable task was to instill both into Soviet society, trying to make them one.[41]

In an interview with *Der Spiegel*, Afanasyev expanded upon some other themes relevant to Memorial. At first he explained why the state would not grant Memorial the kind of independence that is so essential to the movement. He believed that the state had almost a "sixth sense" that the movement not only did not suit it but even threatened it.[42] He expressed the hope for more attention and respect from the Party, which would be interpreted as a great step toward getting out of the "morass of Stalinism."[43] Afanasyev also directed other comments toward the Party. Memorial had requested that restitution for the victims and their families come not only from the State but also from the Party, as a way of "assuming responsibility for what happened."[44] Afanasyev added that he could not imagine a more concrete expression of this responsibility than for the Party to directly provide material compensation to victims. On the trial issue, the co-chairman asserted that Memorial was definitely against the Nuremberg Tribunal model of individual trials, going on to explain that since Stalinism had deep roots in the thoughts and attitudes of the Soviets, there would be too many Stalinists to try.[45] This was also one of Sakharov and Bonner's main arguments against such a proceeding.

From his historian's perspective, Afanasyev talked about the importance of archives in the Soviet Union. He recommended the full opening of public archives and libraries as a way of overcoming the "post-Stalinist command system."[46] In that way, the past would be accessible to everyone. Moreover, historians should be able to work in all archives, he asserted. If archives are reserved for chief ideologists and chief historians, he pointed out, history would be made in Party and Central Committee conferences and history would continue to be utilized as an ideological and propaganda instrument. But even when the archives are opened, Afanasyev continued, that will not reveal the whole truth because a lot of what happened—for example, the passing of death sentences—was not documented. Much has to be reconstructed. This is where Memorial can and is playing a great role.[47] Afanasyev stressed the value of utilizing oral history for recording memories and putting together a public archive. Included also would be manuscripts, letters and other materials.[48] Afanasyev envisioned Memorial ultimately following this sequence: getting stories directly from the people, giving them back to the people, finding out correct numbers and making awareness of events and their consequences a part of everyday life.[49] In its two years of existence, Memorial was already indisputably instilling a new awareness, breaking through mindsets that took seventy years to build.

NOTES

1. *Nedelya* 48, 1988.
2. *Vesti s Ukraini*, 15 December 1988.
3. Ibid.
4. *Sovetskaya Kultura*, 27 December 1988.
5. *Reuters*, 27 December 1988.
6. Ibid.
7. Oleg Orlov, interview held at his Moscow home, April 10, 1990.
8. Moscow World Service in English (Radio Liberty file), 31 December 1988.
9. *AP*, 27 December 1988.
10. Ibid.
11. *Reuters*, 27 January 1989.
12. *New York Times*, 28 December 1988.
13. *Washington Post*, 27 December 1988.
14. Ibid.
15. *Agence France Presse*, 15 January 1989.
16. *USSR Today, Soviet Media Features Digest*, compiled by Radio Liberty, Munich, 2 February 1989.
17. *Washington Post*, 30 January 1989.
18. *New York Times*, 29 January 1989.
19. Press release of speech excerpts from the Memorial Founding Conference press center, Moscow, January 1989.
20. *Deutsche Presse Agentschaft*, 28 January 1989.
21. *New York Times*, 29 January 1989.
22. Press release, Memorial Founding Conference press center, Moscow, January 1989.
23. Ibid.
24. *Reuters*, 28 January 1989.
25. Press release, Memorial press center, January 1989.
26. Ibid.
27. Ibid.
28. Ibid.
29. The All-Union Memorial's Charter remained in this form until the dissolution of the Soviet Union. Despite amendments made thereafter, the essence of the Society's goals did not change. Moreover the original version of the Charter remains relevant because it addresses the issues of the period examined in this book and helps us to better understand both the context and the salience of Memorial.

30. *Ogonyok* 6, 1989.
31. *Reuters*, 29 January 1989.
32. *Washington Post*, 30 January 1989.
33. *Baltimore Sun*, 30 January 1989.
34. Robert E. Pittinger, Charles S. Hockett, John J. Danehy, *The First Five Minutes* (Ithaca, NY: Paul Martineau, 1960), p. 234.
35. *Novoye Vremya* 6, 1989.
36. *XX Century and Peace*, February 1989.
37. *Moscow News* 6, 5 February 1989.
38. Ibid.
39. Ibid.
40. Ibid.
41. Ibid.
42. *Der Spiegel* (Germany), 13 February 1989.
43. Ibid.
44. Ibid.
45. Ibid.
46. Ibid.
47. Ibid.
48. Ibid.
49. Yuri Afanasyev, interview held in Amsterdam, May 10, 1990.

CHAPTER 6 _____

1989–1990: Memorial Branches Out

In the aftermath of the Founding Conference, Memorial started to expand in many directions, gaining support as well as encountering opposition. In either event it was gaining recognition from both its own activities and from press coverage. Newspapers like *Komsomolskaya Pravda* were printing readers' letters inquiring about Memorial. On March 5, 1989, Memorial held a public "meeting" in Moscow devoted to the "consecutive de-Stalinization of society." The resolutions, bearing close resemblance to a political platform, were clearly a campaign effort for the approaching March 26 elections. The opening lines are familiar Memorial sentiments:

We express the hope that the bureaucracy does not manage to extinguish the vivid spirit of our movement, to silence or misrepresent its humanistic nature and goals. Memorial will exist as an exposure of Stalinism, as a pang of conscience to the people, as a summons to vigilance against new crimes.[1]

The demands that followed contain much stronger language and were made with reference to "victims of Stalinism and Brezhnevism." The first demand was that the crimes of Stalinism be recognized as "crimes against humanity" and genocide; against all that is "progressive, active and moral in a people"; and should be dealt with as such, according to the International Convention of 1968.[2] Furthermore, Memorial complained here that the punitive apparatus, instead of being curbed, was being increased. It cited events in Vilnius and Minsk, the arrest of members of the Karabakh Committee and other such repressions. Additionally, it called for the draft of the law on State Security to be presented for public discussion and referendum. This list of demands did not limit itself to the Soviet Union's internal affairs; it also addressed the country's external activities. One such issue was the necessity for the Soviet state to acknowledge its responsibility for the existence of "brutal Stalinist regimes" in North Korea, Ethiopia, and Romania as well as other countries. Memorial asked the government to refuse to cooperate with these and other regimes associated with mass repressions. The resolutions of this "meeting" concluded with a plea to oppose those connected with crimes of Stalinism, the Brezhnev nomenklatura, demagogy, deceit, blackmail or intimidation in the March 26 elections.[3] These resolutions were beginning to resemble a democratic platform, and Memorial's stance looked more and more political.

During this period, Memorial was undergoing philosophical changes as well as a physical growth. Events unimaginable just a year earlier were coming to pass. An article in *Komsomolskaya Pravda* described a meeting that took place between the Karaganda section of Memorial and Ministry of Internal Affairs (MVD) officials who worked in the Karaganda camp complex in the 1930s, 1940s and 1950s. The Memorial group was trying to gain access to camp records. It wanted to know the conditions that existed in the camp for political prisoners, their numbers and their identity. The meeting was, however, to no avail. The existence of political prisoners was virtually denied; the "good treatment" the prisoners received was emphasized; the existence of mass graves was ignored; and the former MVD officials even boasted that many freed prisoners settled in Karaganda, "so warmed were their hearts to the camps that they didn't have the strength to part."[4] This was a disappointing but not altogether surprising response from the former MVD officials. Still, attempts continued. The former camp workers announced that a meeting would take place between themselves and former prisoners of the "Karlag." This event did not occur totally without incident. The former MVD officials demanded a stop to the publication of a number of articles on the Karlag in *Industrialnaya Karaganda*, claiming they were undermining the authority of the MVD and turning people against the Party. One of the former MVD men threatened to shoot Y. Kuznetsova, the journalist responsible, if he "had only had a gun."[5] Though Memorial did not receive an honest disclosure from the MVD, the fact that such a meeting took place at all was already a significant return for its efforts. Memorial had come a long way since 1987. It also had a long way to go.

The first weekend of March 1989 witnessed two major events in Ukraine—the founding conference of the All-Ukrainian Memorial Society on March 4 and a related anti-Stalinist rally attended by 1,500 people on the anniversary of Stalin's death, March 5. Similar to the Moscow Memorial, the Ukrainian Memorial's founding conference took place in the Cinematographers Union building in Kiev. It was attended by delegates from twenty-five Ukrainian regions, representatives of the unofficial Ukrainian Orthodox Church, the banned Ukrainian Catholic Church, the Ukrainian Helsinki Union, the Society of Moscow Ukrainians "Slavutich" and, according to its spokesman Anatoly Dosenko, American and French diplomats. A broadcast on Radio Free Europe/Radio Liberty outlined the society's resolutions. Though they shared the All-Union Society's goals, the Ukrainian society was more politicized. Radio Liberty reported: "participants of the conference accepted an organizational charter and a number of resolutions in which the social-political platform of the society was crystallized."[6] A representative of this Memorial called it "one more oasis of democracy in Ukraine."[7] Although the Ukrainian resolutions begin with a confirmation of the January 29 All-Union Founding Conference resolutions, later points contain a more distinctly political tone. They request that the Ukrainian Procuracy, KGB and Ministry of Internal Affairs provide needed support for local Memorial chapters. With regard to the "campaign of discreditation" conducted by the mass media, they suggest an appropriate corrective. At the conclusion of research into the activities carried out by Ukrainian "participants in mass repression" (from the 1920s to the 1980s), they suggest that same mass media publish the results. The subjects of investigation should include members of state institutions during the repressive times of Brezhnev. The Ukrainian Memorial went even further and called for the opening of the archives of the Ministry of Internal Affairs, the Ministry of State Security and the KGB which contain documents on the suppression of the 1920s and 1930s. The group requested that a petition concerning the law on state secrets be presented to the USSR Supreme Soviet, specifically demanding that the Soviet state comply with international practices.

The following section of the resolutions contains even more direct demands with reference to Ukrainian human rights defenders. It begins with the request that friends and families of prisoners of conscience, people like Vasily Stus and others, who died in captivity, be given the opportunity to return to their homeland. This return should coincide with the publication of their works. As for those who survived, their sentences should be withdrawn, they should be rehabilitated, and they should be given material compensation.[8] The Ukrainian Memorial also addressed the issue of the prevalent abuse of psychiatry for political purposes. They vowed to seek the abolition of this practice and the release of the pedagogue Anatoly Ilchenko from psychiatric prison. They expressed the need for a monument to commemorate those who died in Kharkov in the 1932–1933 state-engineered famine. Monuments should also be constructed in Bykovnya and other mass grave sites in Ukraine. In conjunction with all this, the Society asserted that the Ukrainian Catholic and Orthodox churches should be legalized. The exhibits at this meeting included a list of Ukrainian writers killed in the 1930s and 1940s, and a poster depicting the mass grave at Bykovnya.[9]

At a rally in front of a Kiev stadium the following day, on the anniversary of Stalin's death, many of the same issues were raised and shouts from the public of "Stalin lives" could be heard.[10] The deputy chief of the Kiev Communist Party was in attendance. His support for the call to open the archives drew enthusiastic applause. His statement that the Party itself was a victim of Stalin brought little applause and less sympathy. The rally fell, significantly, in the midst of campaigns for the upcoming March 26 elections. Four "democracy activists" were jailed on "hooliganism" charges.[11] The rally was also attended by a significant number of KGB agents, confirming the underlying disharmony between the Ukrainian Party leadership under Vladimir Shcherbitsky and democratic and nationalist-oriented groups.[12]

On that same day, another such meeting was taking place in Moscow— its orientation: anti-Stalin, anti-Ligachev, pro-Yeltsin. At the meeting, initiated by Memorial in Gorky Park, a gathering of 2,000 people applauded calls by Yuri Karyakin and others asking for the Politburo conservative Yegor Ligachev to step down. The public were mindful of the neo-Stalinist article by a Leningrad teacher, Nina Andreyeva, that was published the previous year while Gorbachev was away and Ligachev asserted Party ideology. Ligachev, associated with conservative resistance to reform, was believed to be using his executive post in agriculture to impede efforts to reshape Soviet agriculture by changing the collective farming system.[13] Memorial passed a resolution, endorsed by the crowd, supporting candidates in the upcoming election who condemned Stalin's crimes and were not part of Brezhnev's nomenklatura, the Party and government elite. The group was unified in its support of Boris Yeltsin, who had complained that the pace of reform was moving too slowly. Yevgeny Yevtushenko spoke to the gathering about the Stalinist-type repressions still continuing in Byelorussia in the form of resistance to the commemoration of purge victims.[14] Other speakers presented resolutions from Memorial's Founding Conference and were applauded. Surveying the different groups of reformers present, one journalist commented, "the rally showed how Memorial was uniting a wide range of progressives and radicals into what amounts to an embryonic opposition party, a phenomenon feared by the Communist party apparat (bureaucracy)."[15]

But Memorial was not the only group marking the 36th anniversary of Stalin's death on March 5. While Memorial was holding its rally in Gorky Park, Pamyat (Memory), an ultra-Right, Russian nationalist organization associated with anti-Semitism, was placing a wreath on Stalin's grave in Red Square. In the words of Arseny Roginsky, historian and member of Memorial's Scientific Council:

There are two movements fighting for the soul of Russia: Pamyat and Memorial. . . . One could say that the two movements for historical memory roughly represent something of the eternal struggle of the Slavophiles and the Westernizers in Russian life, in that Pamyat is singularly Russian nationalist to the point of anti-Semitism and xenophobia, while Memorial has a liberal international perspective and counts many Jews and other minorities among its leading activists.[16]

Whereas Memorial includes cultural figures and intellectuals, Pamyat is made up of discontented youths and many workers, who, frustrated with the declining standard of living, blame the disorder on democratization.[17] Thus, Memorial was confronted with resistance both from the state and from some fellow citizens who may have had the implicit backing of official conservative forces. The opening up of Soviet society under Gorbachev brought social forces of many stripes to the surface. One of Memorial's greatest tasks remains to convince people that it is not the process of change and democratization that has brought on the current crisis. Quite the contrary, the crisis is the chaos consequent to the fall of a flawed economic, political and spiritual system. Strong democratic institutions, such as Memorial, are its best hope for rehabilitation.

When Stalin died, he left a legacy of mass graves to the Soviet people. The anniversary of his death was commemorated in a variety of ways. On that day Mikola Lysenko, a retired economist and Memorial member, was exploring the notorious Bykovnya mass grave site outside of Kiev. It was marked only by a pink granite slab bearing the Ukrainian inscription, "An eternal memorial to the 6,329 people buried here: soldiers, partisans and peaceful citizens tortured and killed by the fascist occupiers between 1941 and 1943." It lay behind a high green fence and guard house, put up half a century ago.[18] The official story claiming German responsibility for the atrocities was more or less maintained despite a number of investigative commissions. In 1989, though, witnesses, emboldened by official and unofficial efforts at de-Stalinization, came forward to challenge the official story. They averred that four years before the Germans arrived, tarpaulin-covered trucks were depositing their cargo here. The witnesses had no doubt that it was the work of Stalin's Secret Police.[19] Estimates of the dead at this particular site range from as low as 1,329 to as high as 240,000—the latter figures were put forward by Lysenko who paced off the space and calculated how many bodies could fit.

The first commission to investigate the matter was a 1944 war crimes commission. After the Red Army's recapture of Kiev in 1943, villagers desperately seeking firewood pulled down the fence. The eerie clue that something was amiss was the sight of grass where it had never grown before.[20] Predictably, the commission, under the restrictive Stalinist state, concluded that it must have been the work of the Nazis. A second commission was formed in 1971 after the area was vandalized by scavengers in search of wedding rings and gold teeth.[21] The conclusion was the same. A third commission was formed to study the matter after Lysenko had collected the testimony of ten elderly villagers in 1987. The conclusion was unaltered, but the pink granite memorial was put up in May 1987. Lysenko, dissatisfied with this verdict, gathered more witnesses, and in December of that year a fourth commission was set up. Some eyewitnesses told of how the Nazis unearthed the bodies during excavations in 1941 and took photographs. According to one villager, "By 1942, they had found thousands of bodies. The evidence was published in the press, as proof of Stalin's atrocities."[22]

Lysenko was convinced that under pressure from Memorial the truth would finally be revealed. His prediction proved to be correct. In February 1990, a stone dedicated to "the victims of Stalinist terror" was placed on the grounds of the October Palace in Kiev. This was the site of the 1930s NKVD headquarters where many victims buried in Bykovnya were executed.[23] Memorial also succeeded in obtaining grudging official acknowledgment of NKVD culpability at Kuropaty, near Minsk, and Katyn Forest, near Smolensk. If we consider the enormous effort required to expose the official cover-up of Bykovnya as a typical example of the official amnesia that pervaded the Soviet Union, then we see the significance of Memorial's accomplishment. In a relatively short time span, Memorial had succeeded in discrediting some of the myths on which so many new lies were based. However, a later development gives this Bykovnya story a worrisome twist. In August 1990 the stone, perhaps too discomfiting a reminder to the Party or KGB, disappeared.[24] Change comes hard and is hard to sustain.

The following month witnessed a Memorial exhibition in Moscow, as well as the creation of new regional Memorial divisions. Activities of local societies in such places as the Urals, Tallinn, Kalinin (campaigning at the time to become the "Tver" Memorial), Tomsk, Sverdlovsk and Tkvaricheli (Georgia) were reported in local papers. *Vecherny Tallinn*, for example, carried a front-page article entitled, "The Living Need It . . ." This story was about a section of the city's Memorial that concentrated on repressed chess players, and it asked readers to send any relevant information they might have.[25] In Moscow, Memorial was one of the supporters of an unsanctioned meeting on the Arbat protesting the violence used against demonstrators in Tbilisi. Andrei Sakharov, Yuri Karyakin and Andrei Voznesensky spoke at the gathering.

Moscow's "Week of Conscience" in November of the previous year was a ground-breaking event. By April 1989 the ground had been sufficiently prepared in other cities for a similar event to take place. A report from Sverdlovsk announced the successful completion of arrangements for the Week.[26] In Leningrad, the local Memorial, together with the Cultural Foundation, arranged for the event to be held in the Leningrad Palace of Culture from April 5 to April 11, 1989. The entrance was marked by an exhibition displaying a map of the Gulag and designating seventy-two of the camps used from 1918 to the present. Monument proposals as well as a Wall of Remembrance could also be found there. More than 6,000 rubles were raised from ticket sales and contributions to the fund for remembrance. Leningrad's Week followed the same basic structure as Moscow's, having different themes for different days. On one occasion, reactions to a historian's speech, "The Red Terror in Petrograd," illustrated the still contentious nature of the de-Stalinization process. Some in the audience, still faithful to Lenin's ideas, shouted for the speaker to get off the stage, while others applauded him. Another presentation was made by history student Dmitry Yurasov who had just come from L'vov's "Week of Conscience." He reported on various statistics he had researched. For example, he found that hundreds of thousands of people of fifty-five nationalities (and eighteen nations) were deported to the East. Roundtable discussions centered on religious persecution and the persecution of artists in the 1920s, 1930s and 1940s.

On the final day, more recent forms of repression were discussed under the theme "Stalin Died?" Veniamin Iofe, an engineer and one of the five co-chairmen of the Leningrad Memorial, spoke about political repressions of small-scale (amateur) groups from 1953 to 1969. Iofe could speak from experience. He himself had been convicted in the "Kolokol affair" during this period. As part of an illegal Marxist group, he had helped found the organ *Kolokol*, wrote articles for it and disseminated it. The articles centered on themes like "reforms" and "The First Steps of the New Government." Iofe was tried under Articles 70-1 (anti-Soviet agitation and propaganda) and 72 of the Criminal Code of the RSFSR by the Leningrad City Court. He was charged with membership and active participation in an illegal organization, to which he pleaded guilty. Iofe was sentenced to three years of camp and interned in Mordovian Camp 1.[27] In his presentation to the gathering, Iofe said that he considered such organizations not so much real political groups but "resistance" groups.[28] He is one of the few historians to focus on this particular period. Short of state archives, source material on the period before 1961 was hard to come by, so he had to seek other methods.[29] People who knew of Iofe's activities and interests suggested that he join Memorial and start working on oral history. That is exactly what he did. In the next chapter, we will return to both Veniamin Iofe and oral history.

The late spring of 1989 brought new challenges to Memorial. The worldwide attention its activities had begun to receive was not coming only from the West. In a letter dated April 17, 1989, Charter 77, the Czechoslovak human rights movement, addressed the Memorial society in Moscow in an effort to draw attention to its own Stalinist era. It pointed out that Stalinism had many advocates in Czechoslovakia and still continued to flourish. Charter 77 wanted to work in cooperation with Memorial in setting up a joint East European seminar on Stalinism. The letter explained that in Poland a commission had already been created to study "victims of the Stalinist period repression"; Hungary was planning to open up archives on show trials between 1945 and 1962; and Bulgarian leader Todor Zhivkov was blaming Stalin for the death of over 600 Bulgarian communists.[30] The letter complained of the country's loss of historical awareness and the distorted curriculum in schools, a familiar issue for the Moscow-based historical enlightenment society. By facilitating the collaboration between many separate organizations, Memorial was giving a voice and a stage to a common problem, an issue that touched so many lives in so many ways. But its role was not always acknowledged.

A news report in May 1989 on informal organizations from Alma-Ata was conspicuous in its omission of Memorial. The only "informal" organization that successfully developed in Kazakhstan was "Nevada"—a movement to stop nuclear testing in Kazakhstan and throughout world.[31] At that time, according to Arseny Roginsky, the situation in Alma-Ata was very complicated. At first, Memorial's existence there was permitted, but later the authorities banned it.[32] At the same time, a Memorial branch formed in the city of Khabarovsk, 5,000 miles and seven time zones away from Moscow. Such places are particularly important for Memorial since they were major centers of the prison camp network, or Gulag Archipelago, in the Far East.[33] Some local newspapers have helped to inform their readers of the area's history. They published maps of Stalin's labor camps along the BAM Railway, a trans-Siberian route, as well as descriptions of slave laborers' ordeals. The local Memorial branch in Khabarovsk has set goals for itself such as locating the burial places of Stalin's victims and identifying and bringing to justice any surviving Stalinist henchmen of the 1930s. It has also set out to change Soviet street names, like Karl Marx Avenue, back to their original Russian names—in this case, Nikolai Muraviev Street, named after the Tsarist general who founded this city in 1858.[34] That same month, in the north, Arkhangelsk established its local branch of Memorial, naming it Sovest (Conscience).[35]

In the meantime, Memorial was flexing its political muscles. Telman Gdlyan, who became known for his exposure of corrupt officials, among them the leadership of Soviet Uzbekistan and Brezhnev's son-in-law Yuri Churbanov, found himself under investigation for "serious violation of laws" while gathering information. Though it was officially prohibited, Memorial organized a rally in Moscow's Gorky Park on May 7, 1989, in order to give Gdlyan the chance to tell his side of the story, an opportunity denied to him by the official media. He was detained, however, by plainclothes policemen and thus did not manage to address the hundreds gathered by Memorial.[36] Memorial activists continued their support of Gdlyan's actions.

Elsewhere, four members of Memorial, together with thirty sympathizers, were sentenced to fifteen days in prison for trying to participate in an official May Day rally in Gorky. They went on a hunger strike in protest. May Day found Memorialers in many cities with signs like: "Get rid of Article 6 of the Constitution." Memorial members in Rostov were also confronted with litigious if not authentically legal proceedings. Both cases illustrate the resistance that Memorial members in the provinces were facing.[37] But this was not the case everywhere. There were still many places where Memorial was able to flourish. Arseny Roginsky explained that in the absence of official status, Memorial was not keeping membership records, but it was obvious that the organization was growing. He reported that a 50,000-person stadium in Minsk was filled to capacity for a Memorial meeting. Memorial gatherings in Ukraine could also boast many supporters: 5,000 attended meetings in Kiev, while attendance in L'vov tripled this figure. In Kharkov, daily articles on Memorial and other informal organizations appeared in the press. Nevertheless, Roginsky was unambiguous in his assertion that Memorial "is not a political movement. [We] support [then] General Secretary Gorbachev . . . we are against the abuse of power, not against communism. We are trying to help perestroika and are not seeking power."[38] Still, many do not share his point of view. One of Roginsky's claims is, however, undisputed:

The greatest success of Memorial so far is the fact that these groups in different cities managed to find each other, managed to unite, managed to express common goals and, nevertheless, managed, despite all the difficulties (and there were many), to achieve and conduct a Founding Conference. People in entirely different parts of the country united around a very important idea, and finally, it seems, may start working toward its realization in the framework of society, and not only within the framework of an informal union.[39]

Memorial and other informal organizations received official permission to hold a preparatory meeting for the coming Congress of People's Deputies. Some of the deputies took part in the May 21, 1989, gathering at the Luzhniki. Many of the speakers expressed the hope that the purview of the Congress could expand enough to encompass key legislative questions, economics, and the strengthening of the legal foundations of government. A strong protest was voiced concerning the serious transgression of the law on the part of the investigators of the USSR Procuracy in the Telman Gdlyan and Nikolai Ivanov case. It was suggested that this task be delegated to a new commission appointed by the Congress.[40] A preparatory congress in Leningrad, attended by 1,000 people, gave a "mandate" to the People's Deputies of Leningrad calling for the release of the names of the special task force troops of the Soviet Army responsible for violent reprisals on peaceful demonstrators in Tbilisi. These relatiatory actions were the official answer to the students' request for more democratization and greater autonomy from the central authority of Moscow. The mandate called for criminal charges to be brought against the troops. The gathering also demanded the dismissal of Soviet Defense Minister Dmitry Yazov.[41] It is difficult to maintain that this type of activity was not political. Such activities were as much a part of Memorial as the historical enlightenment work, though they were led by a different group within the organization.

A similar pre-Congress rally in Gorky Park, attended by 3,000, was organized by Memorial on May 23, 1989. Issues raised included the Gdlyan Ivanov affair, which may implicate Yegor Ligachev, and restitution of citizenship for figures like Vladimir Bukovsky (exiled in the 1970s). Roginsky and others protested that official efforts to eradicate Stalinism and rehabilitate its victims were thus far insufficient.[42]

Around this time the Novosibirsk Memorial sent an open letter to Soviet Politburo member Ligachev regarding a mass grave discovered in the Tomsk region in 1979. He had been Party leader of the region at the time.

In 1979 when the Ob river flooded the site of a former NKVD prison, it unleashed a torrent of mummified corpses. The KGB eliminated all traces of this finding.[43] Memorial demanded that those responsible for the cover-up be punished, pointing out that concealing crimes was a criminal act.[44]

By the end of May 1989, in Murmansk, hitherto extraordinary events were taking place. The Murmansk provincial committee of the CPSU and the leadership of the Murmansk provincial KGB were cultivating contact with informal organizations. Consequently, the Murmansk Memorial society met with local KGB leaders to discuss the rehabilitation of victims repressed during the Stalin era. A roundtable discussion was held in which historians, journalists and lawyers took part. The discussion centered on opening archives, both those of the NKVD and materials that were in the possession of the KGB leadership. It was agreed that they would help Memorial in their search for camp sites as well as prisons.[45] The times were certainly changing.

An increasing awareness of Stalinism and its consequences was penetrating the public consciousness at all levels. Yet, on May 30, 1989, when a member of Memorial stood at Boris Pasternak's grave at Peredelkino and spoke about Pasternak and other victims, the few schoolchildren who happened to be there said that they knew nothing about the poet.[46] There could hardly be a stronger justification for Memorial's historical enlightenment.

June 1989 was another eventful month for Memorial. A Memorial-organized rally at the Luzhniki stadium in Moscow attracted over 20,000 supporters to honor human rights campaigner Andrei Sakharov. Speaker Boris Yeltsin praised the honorary chairman's courage in speaking out against issues such as the Soviet military intervention in Afghanistan, for which Sakharov was banished for a period of seven years.[47] On June 13, 1989, the executive committee of the Leningrad City Council of People's Deputies officially registered the charter of Leningrad's Memorial. The main Administration of Culture, in cooperation with the Social Council and the Board of the Leningrad Memorial, were assigned the task of working out the rules and conditions for an open competition for a monument to the victims of Stalinism. In addition, regional authorities were to approve a location in a central part of the city for the local Memorial, a commission was set up to investigate gravesites of victims of Stalinism, and the chief authorities of finance were instructed to set up a bank account for the Leningrad Memorial. In the province of L'vov, the founding conference of its local chapter of Memorial took place in the Palace of Culture. Despite protests from the local KGB, the Ukrainian national flag was hung at this meeting. The Odessa chapter held its founding conference on June 10, 1989, and adopted a charter declaring its support for both the democratic minority in the Congress of People's Deputies and the Chinese students who became victims of "bloody repression."[48] In Moscow, a Memorial meeting attended by 200 people discussed, among other issues, the recall of a number of People's Deputies. At a gathering of the Irkutsk Memorial, chairman Alexander Novikov announced his chapter's support of Gdlyan and Ivanov.[49] Clearly, Memorial was expanding geographically and politically, occupying a wide range of places and occupied with a broad range of issues.

To consolidate its gains, Memorial became increasingly involved with the projects of other organizations that share similar goals. The Moscow Association of Victims of Unlawful Repression, in an article in *Moscow News*, explained that their work was directed toward caring for the victims of Stalin's Terror. They expressed enthusiasm about working together with Memorial as well as with the Russian Orthodox Church.[50] The Association, however, began to be too imitative of Soviet officialdom for Memorial's taste—with their dachas, state support, office in the center of Moscow, and the like, so cooperation between the two organizations is limited.[51] In Donetsk, a Memorial group working with a Jewish center was researching the years of Hitler's occupation in an attempt to compile and publish a list of the names of victims of Nazism.[52] In another case, the majority of the proceeds from an exhibition in honor of Khrushchev were turned over to Memorial.[53]

By July 1989, the mass media was devoting increasing attention to the grisly discoveries of mass graves taking place all over the country. That summer Memorial held a meeting in a park in Donetsk province to discuss the discovery of the "graves" in the Rutchenko fields where bones had been unearthed in a building excavation. In the best tradition of the motif of the grateful dead, Memorial made arrangements for the proper reburial of these victims. They numbered just short of 40,000.[54] On Golden Mountain near Chelyabinsk, where gold was once mined, a trove of a different kind yielded to the spade. The remains of bullet-pierced skulls were found. On a digging expedition, Memorial members discovered at least 350 such victims. Estimates were that no less than 300,000 victims were "buried" in Golden Mountain. Clearly, such places were to be consecrated as significant centers of remembrance. As a "Vremya" correspondent concluded, " 'Golden Mountain,' having preserved secrets for long years, from this day on became a place of sorrow for the Uralers, for the innocent victims of Stalinist henchmen."[55] In other instances, in a sand quarry at Poltava, Ukraine, the remains of about 5,000 people were found by diggers. These findings were reported in the press about once a month, either as discoveries or reburial ceremonies. From the silence of the grave, the voice of protest was rising.

Oleg Golovanov, Memorial's coordinator of mass grave discovery projects, lamented publicly, "this is a country built on bones."[56] Golovanov estimated that there were approximately 100,000 unmarked mass graves filled by Stalin's purges, repressions and labor camp victims. Digging them up was essential to the aims of exposing the extent of Stalin's evil and posthumously restoring honor to the victims. He went on to say that the bones were also a statement about the country's communist leaders. In the previous month the Central Committee had ordered local governments to cooperate with groups like Memorial and to recognize mass burial places as official cemeteries. The decree also added that the KGB and police should help in this effort. However, the KGB and local governments continued to hinder efforts, according to the Memorial coordinator. NKVD archives that could have helped locate the graves were officially classified as "not in proper condition to be useful," and some of the known sites continued to be set aside for use as garages and houses by local officials. Golovanov pleaded that "people need a place to come and lay flowers."[57] This poignant statement emphasizes a primary objective of Memorial—to revivify a dead history and a history of death, to return to people the right to remember. In August 1989, on the 50th anniversary of the Molotov-Ribbentrop Pact, Memorial held an exhibition on this theme in Moscow. Hundreds attended, and many heard for the first time incriminating details of Soviet complicity with the Nazis.[58]

Meanwhile, Memorial was expanding its activities in another realm— oral history. In the summer of 1989, an expedition of Moscow Historical Archive Institute students went on an oral history fact-finding mission to the Kuban, scene of the 1933 famine. Darya Khubova, at that time a doctoral student at the Institute studying foreign experience in oral history, led the expedition. As documented in an article in *Poisk*, the ancient term "vox populi" took on a different meaning in the climate of the times. It was no longer the din of a faceless multitude mouthing the official line, but the living witnesses and performers of history.[59] Since most of history is in fact the saga of people who occupy an unofficial status, it is critical to hear *their* story. Instead of the anticipated silence of inchoate feelings, before the microphone the subjects were articulate and eager to tell their stories. Erupting from years of pent-up bitterness and in voices quaking with emotion, the survivors answered the students' questions about the Stalin period.[60]

On another search-and-tell mission, Memorial set out to find Mikhail Molovtsov, a former dissident, philosopher, teacher and then mailman in Yeremkovo.[61] As a young Marxist he was arrested in 1958 with three other philosophy students and sentenced to five years in a labor camp for drafting an "anti-Soviet manuscript of programmatic character."[62] He was first sent to Vorkuta and then Mordovia. After release in 1965 Molovtsov retreated to the Russian countryside, where he was rediscovered in 1989 by Memorial. In the spring of 1990, he was elected as a People's Deputy of the Russian Federation (RSFSR), and became part of the Russian Social-Democratic Party and of the bloc "Democratic Russia" as well as a member of the Commission on Human Rights, which is chaired by known dissident Sergei Kovalyov (co-chairman of the All-Union Memorial since June 1990).[63] Clearly, Memorial was shifting its emphasis from reading the text of history to teaching its lessons. In the process, it made some history of its own.

Since oral history was such a new field for Soviet historians, Memorial decided to organize an international conference on the subject on October 3–5, 1989. The conference brought together Memorial members with others from all over the Soviet Union at Moscow's Historical Archive Institute to discuss issues in oral history. Complicated visa problems resulting from Memorial's lack of official recognition reduced the international delegation to a small group of Western specialists—Paul Thompson from England, Selma Leydesdorff and Jaap Talsma from Holland, and Alexander von Plato from (then) West Germany. Eager Memorialers diligently learned the methodology of oral history and how it has been applied in de-Nazification as well as de-Stalinization. At a roundtable discussion, Memorial members and oral history students held lengthy exchanges with the Western historians. The mood was hopeful but also cautious, as Selma Leydesdorff recounted in an article in *De Groene Amsterdammer*: "No one can say at this moment, how all of this is going to end up, as one historian put it: 'We'll just go on, but maybe one day, from a camp in Siberia, we will be writing the story of a conference at a strange time in Moscow when everything seemed possible'."[64]

The conference difficulties illustrated certain organizational problems that are partially due to long Soviet isolation from the West. It suffered from lack of administrative experience. Programs did not fully correspond to speeches. There were too many speakers, and some speeches were too long. The speeches were never published, which made the conference privy to only those in attendance. On the whole, however, the fact that the event took place at all was as important as what actually happened there.

In mid-October 1989, Memorial held a plenum in Moscow attended by almost two hundred representatives from eighty-six cities. They discussed political issues, the situation in the country, and international relations. Resolutions and a petition to the Supreme Soviet were accepted and People's Deputies Andrei Sakharov and Ales Adamovich expressed their willingness to address Gorbachev on the issue of Memorial's registration at a session of the Supreme Soviet. The plenum passed a resolution dedicating Memorial to the rehabilitation of victims of political repression from the pre-Stalin period to the present. Furthermore, Sakharov's suggestion to designate October 15 as a day of remembrance to General Grigorenko (see Epilogue) was honored. Resolutions were also made demanding the reorganization (even abolition) of the KGB and the liberation of the jailed leaders of the "Karabakh" committee. Additionally, the problematic situation in the Ukrainian city of Sumy was discussed. Local Memorial members had already been on a hunger strike there for two weeks to protest a decision made by local authorities to prohibit a demonstration planned by Memorial. The plenum resolved to consider October 30 the "Day of Democratic Action of Memorial," which would involve making a human chain to extend from the KGB's Lubyanka to the Kremlin.[65] A later press release on this action was headlined, "Remember Those Who Died in the Name of Freedom for the Living!!" It went on to explain that October 30, the Day of Political Prisoners, would be regarded in the Soviet Union as a day of remembrance of victims of the totalitarian regime as well as a day of protest and struggle against political repression. It was also the anniversary of the previous year's incident in Minsk, where local authorities carried out reprisals against participants of a peaceful demonstration in remembrance of those executed at Kuropaty.

The "Lubyanka Chain" was made up of 1,500 candle-holding demonstrators, many of whom had hitherto avoided even walking near the building. On this occasion, however, they peacefully surrounded the headquarters of the KGB.[66] Uniformed police officers were also present, taking pictures while Memorial members distributed leaflets calling for the conversion of the KGB headquarters into a museum to "victims of political terrorism in the Soviet Union."[67] Though protest signs with the names of 100 remaining political prisoners were confiscated, the demonstration continued for the pre-arranged thirty minutes and the gathering dispersed when Memorial declared it over. Those demonstrators who, perhaps provocatively, headed for Pushkin Square were arrested and beaten by special troops.[68] A similar rally was held at Kuropaty, where clergymen conducted services at the mass gravesite.

Andrei Sakharov, the honorary chairman of Memorial, struggled un-
ceasingly for the cause up until the day of his unexpected death on
December 14, 1989. Part of the legacy he left Memorial was the resolve
to continue to fight for human rights in spite of sometimes overwhelming
obstacles. Sakharov's importance to Memorial and Memorial's importance to Sakharov were succinctly summarized in a brief exchange between
Yelena Bonner, Sakharov's widow, and Gorbachev. Gorbachev expressed
his condolences, his sense of personal loss, and proposed ways in which
Sakharov's memory would be honored. Yelena Bonner stoically responded, "It would be better to register Memorial."[69] Many of the initial
issues, such as registration, continued to be issues in its early years,
because they remained unresolved. But these did not prevent Memorial
from being active in exhibitions, meetings, rallies and seminars.

There was a seminar in April 1990 on the subject of maps of the Gulag
in preparation for an exhibition on this theme. Memorial members from
all over the Soviet Union came to Moscow's Historical Archive Institute
for two days of discussion on how to portray and present the vast network
of labor camps that was created under Stalin. At the seminar, various
members took the floor to show their renditions of the location and layout
of particular camps. The exhibition was planned for June 1990, but by
early 1991 it still had not taken place. At times, one realizes that appoint-
ments and dates in the Soviet Union do not have the same reliable character
as they have in the West. Memorial will have to alter this cultural style if
it wants to operate more efficiently and to gain more respect for its
programs.

In April 1990 a joint Soviet-Polish exhibition on Katyn displaying
photographs of Polish officers was also a successful event. In fact, the
international commission that led to the official Soviet admission of
culpability at Katyn was clearly so effective that it inspired a newly formed
commission to use that model in its investigation of the fate of Raoul
Wallenberg.[70] The Swedish diplomat, revered for his heroic rescue of
thousands of Hungarian Jews from the Nazis, disappeared into a Stalinist
labor camp after the Red Army capture of Budapest. While the Soviets
asserted that Wallenberg died in 1947, evidence that he was still alive in
the 1950s and 1960s and perhaps even later compelled Soviet authorities
to make prisons and archives more accessible in order to facilitate conclu-
sive examination of the case.[71] Such an investigation called for a unique
combination of people from different walks of Soviet life. Consequently
a commission was formed from representatives of Soviet law enforcement
and intelligence agencies, former political prisoners, a member of

Moscow's Jewish community, and not surprisingly, someone from Memorial (Arseny Roginsky).

Journalist Bill Keller, in an article on the Arctic city of Vorkuta, describes it as a place where "Stalin transformed free thinkers into coal miners."[72] The problems of yesterday and today mix uncomfortably in this working class community. Stanislav Grintsyavicius, a local resident, has been trying to tend anonymous graves near the Yuroshar Coal Mine. He calls them his "battleground against forgetting."[73] He has been unsuccessful in getting a donation of cement to anchor a memorial cross. Grintsyavicius complains that "People here have gone directly from fear to indifference."[74] Not entirely. While the people of Vorkuta, many of whom came for "premium wages rather than penal servitude,"[75] may seem indifferent to the mass graves beneath their feet, they are nevertheless politically active on other issues. The Vorkuta miners were among the first to seek political concessions such as an end to the Communist Party monopoly on political rule. In contrast, striking miners in Russia and Ukraine were demanding refrigerators and soap.[76] The two causes did unite, however, when the Vorkuta branch of Memorial, whose membership contained more than 1,000 surviving camp victims still living in the city, combined forces with striking miners in the 1990 local elections and ousted Communist Party loyalists from the city council. Reflecting Grintsyavicius's sentiment, local Memorial chairman Vitaly A. Troshin pointed out that "official resistance is no longer an obstacle." But the same could not be said for public indifference.[77] Still, Memorial's efforts to remold a public consciousness shaped by decades of fear continue, sometimes with the help of other organizations. The Vorkuta Historical Museum devoted a room to camp life, displaying, for example, posters from prison camp theatrical productions, a dramatic reminder of the prominent actors and singers who played roles in both these camp shows and the real-life tragedy. Additionally, Ernst Neizvestny, who designed Khrushchev's tombstone, started working on the design for a memorial that will overlook the first prison camp site by the River Vorkuta.

On October 30, 1990, thousands of mourners bearing candles and photographs of lost loved ones gathered across from the Lubyanka in Moscow to commemorate and witness the unveiling of the national monument to "victims of the totalitarian regime." A stone was brought by Memorial from the notorious Solovetsky island labor camp, opened under Lenin in 1918. It was an appropriate symbol—the stark grayness of the victims' lives embodied in the implacable substance of stone. Indeed, it was not the rock that had to be sculpted to construct this monument, it was public consciousness. Oleg Volkov, who survived the Solovetsky camp and twenty-eight years of camp and prison, together with Father Gleb Yakunin, a former political prisoner and member of Parliament, unveiled the monument.[78] Volkov's declamation, "I never thought I would see the day when the truth could be told, and to see a monument to all those who will never return,"[79] speaks poignantly of the enormity of Memorial's accomplishment. The Moscow City Council granted this particular site appropriately across from the KGB, no doubt to the chagrin of many of those who look out onto it.[80]

Despite such a significant victory, official resistance still remained an obstacle to particular local divisions of Memorial and to the All-Union Society Memorial. In the second half of the 1980s Memorial established itself, achieved a broad base of popular support, raised public and official consciousness, and contributed to the comfort of individual survivors' lives, even if only as a compassionate listener to bear witness to stories that must be told. But as it entered the 1990s, Memorial was still burdened by chronic problems. The building in which the All-Union Society first expected to house its Scientific Research Center, archive and museum complex got "lost" in bureaucratic entanglement, so Memorial had to continue to utilize the homes of its members to store the vast amount of new information arriving daily. Furthermore, without official registration, Memorial did not have access to the All-Union Society's bank account. But this did not circumscribe options as much as it might have seemed, since local registered societies could withdraw funds. Clearly, these were not the only obstacles Memorial faced. Public apathy, divergent trends within the organization itself, and the unstable situation in the Soviet Union of that time all threatened to hinder the success of Memorial. Nevertheless, in the spirit of perseverance bequeathed by Andrei Sakharov, monuments to victims of Stalinism were being constructed and the different parts of Memorial continued working toward their common goals. The next chapter provides an opportunity to explore the inner workings of Memorial. It will focus on Memorial's methods of collecting information; how it works in contact with victims; the Scientific Research Center, which processes information; and what Memorial says about itself in conversations and publications.

NOTES

1. Memorial Meeting resolution, 5 March 1989.
2. Ibid.
3. Ibid.
4. *Komsomolskaya Pravda*, 3 March 1989.

5. *Ogonyok* 17, 1989.

6. Resolutions of the Founding Conference of the Ukrainian Memorial, March 10, 1989.

7. Ibid.

8. Ibid.

9. Ibid.

10. *AP* (Kiev), 5 March 1989.

11. Ibid.

12. *Independent* (London), 6 March 1989.

13. *Reuters*, 5 March 1989.

14. Ibid.

15. *Baltimore Sun*, 6 March 1989.

16. *Nyeformaly: Civil Society in the USSR* (New York: Helsinki Watch, 1990), pp. 75–76.

17. *Washington Post*, 6 March 1989.

18. *New York Times*, 6 March 1989.

19. Ibid.

20. *Independent* (London), 10 March 1989.

21. Ibid.

22. Ibid.

23. *Commentary*, (New York) 6 December 1990.

24. Ibid.

25. *Vecherny Tallinn*, 30 March 1989.

26. Radio Liberty (Soviet Media News Budget), April 9, 1989.

27. S. P. de Boer, E. J. Driessen, H. L. Verhaar, *Biographical Dictionary of Dissidents in the Soviet Union, 1956–1975* (The Hague: Martinus Nijhoff, 1982), p. 193.

28. *Russkaya Mysl*, 28 April 1989.

29. Veniamin Iofe, interview held at his home in Leningrad, April 17, 1990.

30. Charter 77, letter to Memorial, April 17, 1989.

31. *Agence France Presse*, 5 May 1989.

32. Radio Liberty report of a broadcast of March 12/13, 1989, *Interview with a member of Memorial's "rabochaya kollegiya," Arseny Roginsky*, May 12, 1989.

33. *Washington Post*, 11 May 1989.

34. Ibid.

35. *Leninskoye Znamya* (Arkhangelsk), 27 May 1989.

36. *Agence France Presse*, 8 May 1989.

37. Ibid., 6 May 1989.

38. *Trouw* (Amsterdam), 17 May 1989.

39. Arseny Roginsky, interview, Radio Liberty, May 12, 1989.

40. *Tass*, 21 May 1989.

41. *Times* (London), 29 May 1989.

42. *Reuters*, 23 May 1989.

    43. Report of telephone interview, Radio Liberty (Munich) Novosibirsk, 23
May 1989.
    44. Yakov Etinger, "History of the Creation, Activity and Problems of Me-
morial," paper (Moscow, 1989), p. 16.
    45. Radio Liberty (Soviet Media News Budget), 29 May 1989.
    46. Soviet Media Features Digest, 30 May 1989.
    47. *CMD* (wire service), 7 June 1989.
    48. *Znamya Kommunisma*, 15 June 1989.
    49. Arkhiv Samizdata, *Radio Liberty Press Bulletin* no. 13, 2 July 1989.
    50. *Moscow News* 29, 1989.
    51. Yakov Etinger, "History."
    52. *Tass*, 24 August 1989.
    53. *Frankfurter Rundschau*, 5 August 1989.
    54. *Pravda*, 4 July 1989.
    55. Radio Liberty (Soviet Media News Budget), 13 September 1989.
    56. *AP*, 15 September 1989.
    57. Ibid.
    58. *Frankfurter Allgemeine Zeitung*, 19 January 1990.
    59. *Poisk*, August 1989.
    60. Ibid.
    61. Laura Starink, "Provincial Mailman Is Now a Member of Parliament,"
NRC Handelsblad (Rotterdam), 19 July 1990.
    62. Ibid.
    63. Ibid.
    64. *De Groene Amsterdammer* (Amsterdam), 14 February 1990.
    65. *Yezhedevnaya Glasnost, Profsoyuz Nezavysimykh*, 18 October 1989.
    66. *Washington Post*, 30 October 1989.
    67. Ibid.
    68. Ibid.
    69. Arseny Roginsky, Bonn, February 8, 1990.
    70. *International Herald Tribune*, 29 August 1990.
    71. Ibid.
    72. Bill Keller, "Taking the Gulag Out of Memory's Deep Freeze," *Interna-
tional Herald Tribune*, 28 August 1990.
    73. Ibid.
    74. Ibid.
    75. Ibid.
    76. Ibid.
    77. Ibid.
    78. *NRC Handelsblad* (Rotterdam), 31 October 1990.
    79. *International Herald Tribune*, 31 October 1990.
    80. Ibid.

PART III _____

MEMORIAL ACTUALIZES ITSELF, HISTORY AS DISSIDENCE

Movements and historical trends appear in retrospect as disembodied forces. But as they emerge they are negotiated and crafted by individuals and grounded in particular events. In this final section, we will present and examine a "bottom-up" view of history. The excesses and early fragmentation of the totalitarian system will be viewed as they were experienced and reported by the victims and by members of Memorial.

CHAPTER 7 _____

Memorial in Action

Every organization, like every individual, may be described from both a diachronic and a synchronic perspective. Developmental history overlaps with, but is also separate from, the current events that are daily negotiated. The historical circumstances of Memorial's development were Stalinism and the liberal reaction to it. As such the role Memorial played in the Soviet system was that of the unwelcome but unavoidable messenger of bad news. But the chronicle of how Memorial got here is not the same as the daily diary of how it works now. For this we will read its news publications, sit in its reception room in Moscow, and interview both the client survivors who come to talk and the member survivors who stay to listen, record and disseminate the accumulating data.

To begin with Memorial's public activities, it organizes meetings, conferences and seminars. In addition, Memorial reaches its audience through newspapers and journals, published by local divisions. One example is *Vedomosti Memoriala*, the All-Union Society's Founding Conference newspaper, which opened with Anna Akhmatova's "Requiem." Since the Founding Conference, similar chronicles have been regularly published by local Memorials in Moscow, Tomsk, Tambov, Leningrad, Arkhangelsk, Kuzbass and other places throughout the Soviet Union. Some are in the form of newsletters, others contain memoirs, platforms of Memorial members campaigning for People's Deputies, open letters to People's Deputies, key speeches from Memorial meetings, articles on historical themes, editorials on current events in the Soviet Union and other national and international topics relevant to Memorial.[1]

Though waiting in line is almost a fixture of Soviet life, it can reasonably be concluded that when people line up, there is something desirable or necessary being offered. The presence of a daily line outside of the (1990) Memorial office at Chernyakovsky 2 (behind the metro station "Aeroport") and the office which replaced it at Maly Karetny Pereulok 12, attests to the fact that there is a demand for what Memorial offers. Just inside the entrance, on the left side of the waiting-room hallway, hangs a bulletin board for use by visitors. The posted messages provide an important social forum and network: "Whoever is interested in going on an expedition to Vorkuta, call . . ."; another note announces a meeting of former Buchenwald prisoners; another asks, "Did anyone know X, last seen in camp Y? Please contact me." Inside the office itself, the wall space is covered by a Memorial information board containing mailboxes for the Memorial leaders as well as for the various divisions within Memorial (Social Council, research center, etc.). Stacks of newspapers reporting on subjects such as "Freedom for Lithuania" are piled deep on the floor, and stacks of questionnaires pile up on the window sills. Its decor is messy but conveys its own functional aesthetic of work in progress. Helping the client/victim to fill out these questionnaires is the first practical step Memorial takes in turning experience into testimony on its way to evidence.

A typical first visit to Memorial's reception room is illustrated by the experience of Vera Ivanovna, a woman whose father and brother died in the camps. She took out a photograph from a plastic bag in which she had preserved letters, documents and other reminiscences, and explained, "This was my brother after he came out of the army. Later he died from cold in a camp. It would have been better if they had just shot them instead of torturing them like that, such a horror."[2] The Memorial associate patiently listened to her story and filled out the form, which asked for particulars about the repressed person such as place of birth, profession, religion, place of residence or date and place of death. In addition, there are more general questions such as: Are there documents relating to the Stalinist period? Does the repressed person need assistance in terms of information about relatives or friends? Legal help? Aid in recording oral history? Date, place and circumstances of arrest; reason for arrest (opinion); where the term was served; release and rehabilitation or refusal thereof. Once completed, this information is filed in Memorial's archives and Vera Ivanovna will probably return regularly to Memorial's reception room, seeking support—legal, social and moral. The reception area is open six days a week for ten hours a day with two volunteers from Memorial present at all times.

Saturday is set aside as legal advice day, bringing together members of Memorial who are lawyers or are well-versed in legal matters in order to provide free advice to victims of Stalinism. What sorts of problems are brought? Galina Moiseyevna's husband was the second secretary of a Party provincial committee who "believed in Stalin." When Galina's husband was arrested in 1938, he made his wife vow not to write to him and told her that she should re-marry. He never returned. Almost twenty years later, in 1957, their son was arrested under Article 58-10 (anti-Soviet agitation). He was sent to a camp in Mordovia, later released and rehabilitated by 1965. One day Galina saw an announcement of a Memorial meeting in the October region of Moscow. She went to find out what it was all about and was impressed when she heard Yevtushenko speak. Later, she read an article by Etinger about his father's alleged involvement in the Doctors Plot. Realizing that she need no longer be alone in her struggle, Galina approached Memorial for help. At eighty years of age, she wanted her son to legally be able to live with her, but this was no easy matter. Through the years she had made two attempts, both unsuccessful, to register her son at her residence. The official refusal was based, no doubt, on her family's "criminal" history, although her husband's case had been reviewed in 1956 and he was posthumously rehabilitated. Galina went to Memorial's office, filled out the questionnaire, provided photos and promised to bring newly available documentation that would help Memorial to establish the legal basis for her son's registration. Some of the official information that she was only recently able to obtain included documents prepared in 1955 and 1956 regarding the fate of her husband.[3]

What, we may ask, is the value of finding out the particulars of a tragic event? What purpose is served by changing the designation of a loved one from "missing person" to "murdered or starved person"? It seems to be in the nature of the way we deal with psychosocial trauma that we cannot optimally get on with the future until we have found a defined place to put the past. Sometimes that involves getting the facts, as in America's post-Vietnam preoccupation with the fate of its MIAs (missing in action). Sometimes it involves retelling one's story until we find an acceptable way of thinking about it and/or an acceptable audience. This psychosocial sequence seems to be a crosscultural phenomenon.

Another Saturday visitor to Memorial was Anna Kasatika, Trotsky's niece, the daughter of his older brother. She recounted how her family was exiled, then brought to camps, then later exiled again, to Kazakhstan. She was released, but her father and brother remained in exile. The relevant information had only recently become available. Anna Alexandrovna Kasatika (formerly Bronstein) could finally find out exactly when her relatives were executed. When she came to Memorial, she was living in a communal apartment and hoped that Memorial could help her to lead a normal life in normal living circumstances.[4] Helping someone move out of a communal apartment situation is more significant than just furnishing comfort and privacy. Memorial historian Nikita Okhotin explained that the concept of communal living, instituted in the 1920s, under which people from different classes and strata of society are forced to live together, creates a terribly unhealthy situation. He asserts that such circumstances were the breeding grounds of the Great Terror. Memorial's efforts aim toward eliminating, wherever possible, the remnants of Stalinism.[5]

Olga Cherepova, a sociologist and coordinator of Memorial's legal assistance group, often works on the Saturday shift. She described some aspects of work in the Moscow Memorial office. On busy days, more than twenty people seek Memorial's assistance. Their requests have focused mainly on receiving compensation for confiscated property and rehabilitation, including restitution, for the period of time they were repressed. In such cases, Memorial can forward the documents supporting a request for a higher pension to the Moscow City Council as well as to People's Deputies. Some of these officials are members of Memorial or at least are favorably disposed toward it. Memorial can also try to aid victims in gaining information about relatives, by providing money and medicine, or attaining privileges like free transport and grocery shopping without waiting in line.[6] Arseny Roginsky pointed out that these people do not have the same status as war veterans, but the moral compensation that they are receiving is one of Memorial's accomplishments.[7]

Memorial offers help to victims or relatives of victims who have suffered repression from 1917 to the present. These include families of peasants who were repressed during collectivization, priests' families, and those who became victims of Soviet psychiatric abuse for political purposes. In the latter case, Memorial refers clients to the Independent Psychiatric Association in Moscow. The clients are examined there and either treated or helped in removing the stigma by receiving psychiatric rehabilitation. Cherepova added that foreign citizens also come for help to Memorial's reception room. Memorial gets letters from places like Poland inquiring into the fate of family members who were deported to the Soviet Union. Other letters ask for help in setting up Memorial-like organizations.[8] One such letter was from the former Deutsche Demokratische Republik (DDR), from Eva-Maria Stege, a woman who had spent 1,729 days and nights in a Soviet labor camp only to be released in 1949 and return to an ever-growing Stalinist presence at home. In the

1950s, Stege was put in pre-trial detention for writing a letter to a colleague in prison. In 1968 she was forbidden to travel, because she did not sign a petition hailing the Soviet invasion of Czechoslovakia.[9]

In the short space of an afternoon visit to Memorial's reception room, my companions and I began to understand one of the main reasons why people need Memorial and, indeed, one of the significant tasks it fulfills. Though the visitors knew of our observer status, that did not prevent them from revealing their entire stories to each of us. Indeed, the pressure in these victims to tell their story was so great that they poured out their hearts to one foreign observer even though they had been informed that he did not understand Russian. Apparently, they were willing to settle for socio-gestural empathy. What we were ear-witnesses to was the effect of decades of silence. During these decades they experienced traumatic events that were at complete variance with both accepted morality and the official description of those events. They suffered in silence. On pain of death the truth that everyone knew could not be told. When such catastrophic events and consequences occur to individuals, it is labelled a post-traumatic stress disorder. Victims have a tendency, unless constrained, to try to cure themselves by ceaseless rumination and spontaneous recounting to almost anyone who will listen. Recollecting her troubled life, Isak Dinesen recalled that sorrows can be borne if you put them into a story or tell a story about them. These people were seeking someone to bear witness to their sorrow. Memorial is sometimes the first witness, but it tries to ensure that it is not the last.

Cherepova explained that for many, the social, moral and legal support that Memorial can provide is compensation enough, but for others the awareness that henchmen are still alive today, and in better condition than their victims, is unbearable and calls for vengeance. She concurred with Sakharov's recommendation that Memorial avoid seeking trials against these henchmen.[10] The court of public opinion might provide both the best punishment for the individual and the best rehabilitation for the system. But not all victims are so bitter, nor do they label themselves as (helpless) victims. As Nikita Okhotin characterized Memorial's Suzanna Solomonovna Pechuro, "she's not a victim, she's a fighter."[11] The way in which Suzanna Solomonovna has processed her experience and turned it to constructive use has made her a fitting role model for those seeking Memorial's support.

Because Suzanna Solomonovna was in eleven prisons (including Lefortovo) and seven camps (including two in the North and Mordovia), she has the sensitivity and motivation to function as coordinator for

Memorial's (initial) 230 local organizations. With such responsibilities, her apartment was necessarily one of the Memorial offices dedicated to preserving part of the already enormous and ever-expanding archive. In a one-year period alone, she and the correspondence committee received thousands of letters from local societies and repressed individuals and responded to all of them! Some ask for answers to specific questions, others for more general information and materials, but "most important," Suzanna asserted, "is to keep up communication with them."[12] Suzanna maintained her home as the reception area for Memorial members until Memorial received its own building. As she discussed her activities, the focus of our conversation shifted fluidly back and forth between Suzanna as a member of Memorial and Suzanna as a former prisoner. The appropriateness of her being in charge of facilitating communication became clear when she disclosed that her worst experience as a prisoner was being alone in a prison for one and a half years: "In a cell alone it is terrible; in a camp you are with others. Her basic optimism, energy and humanism were evident even as she described the bleakness she had endured. "Yes, it was hell and it was terrible but you have to understand," she explained, "these were also very interesting times for us, our interest was greater than our feeling of suffering. . . . We remember it not as horror, but as our experience of youth during which time there were many good things." Suzanna recalled how she had recently run into a former camp-mate as she was preparing for a trip to Irkutsk. He was unable to accompany her but exclaimed, "I envy you, going to Inta, imbibing the air of our youth."

The journey that ended in the camps started in 1948 when she was a high school student. Suzanna had joined a Marxist literary circle. The leader was a young man named Boris whose father had been a Party member. The father was sent to the front in 1941 and subsequently died there. Boris had read and shared many books left by his father, including essays by Marx and Lenin. The circle of students observed that the second edition of Lenin's work was very different from subsequent editions—sections, even photos, were edited out and Lenin's original plans were clearly not being realized. The marked discrepancy between what they were told, what they read (in censured, edited versions) and what they were seeing and experiencing was too great to ignore. Still, they believed in Lenin and the revolution. In hindsight, Suzanna admitted, "We now have a different perspective. Lenin is not an icon, and we understand that everything started with him. That's where our criticism should have begun, not first with 1924." Aware of the riskiness of their activities, the student group began to criticize the system and became a small underground organization. They were subsequently arrested (in 1951) and underwent a seven-day closed trial without defense. Three, including Boris, were shot, and Suzanna received a sentence of twenty-five years. Apparently, somewhat later a large trial to include Suzanna and others was being prepared, but Stalin died and the new issue was dropped. Suzanna was released after five and a half years.

Suzanna said that the camp years were a learning time for her. One of her tasks was to make scarves for supervisors' wives in a workshop. The tediousness of the work was partly alleviated by the richness of her social contact. The woman who worked next to her taught her English. They tried to speak only in English with each other, and after three months, when Suzanna was transferred to the Butyrka prison, she could already read books in English. In the prison, she was given some books but not allowed a dictionary. While she was at camp Suzanna also met a young male student with whom she illicitly corresponded. He encouraged her to study and instilled in her a spirit of pride. Defiantly, he asserted, "they want to turn us into livestock, but we won't let them." To this day, Suzanna believes it is essential for others to understand that although there was grief and suffering and bitterness, there was also humor and pride; "it is true that people walked around, frightened, in silence or in tears, but not completely true. . . . Not everyone was afraid, many people remained human beings— wrote poems, read books." Suzanna considers that her years as a prisoner gave her the opportunity to meet many people. "God probably gave me the task of remembering everything and later telling others about it," she reflected. Suzanna was released in April 1956. Shortly thereafter she passed examinations in English and German at the Historical Archive Institute, and she was already enrolled at the university by September 1956.

Suzanna Solomonovna had heard about Memorial's signature campaign and read a newspaper article on the organization by Yakov Etinger, whom she remembered meeting in 1952 at Kirov transit prison. Consequently, she was one of the earliest to join Memorial, registered as number 28. One of her tasks is to send money to those in need—money collected from exhibitions, donations and honoraria. As part of its charitable work Memorial also sends money to Armenian refugees, hospitals, and, cautiously, in its initial years, some politically delicate causes including Lithuanian independence. Suzanna described Memorial as a "union of all those who want change."

Memorial members often play a dual role in the organization. Memorial provides a place to come for support in seeking reconciliation with one's own past and also a place to utilize one's own experience and talent to help others. Valentina Alexandrovna Tikhanova, like Suzanna Solomonovna

Pechuro, has such a dual relationship to Memorial. As a graduate of Moscow University in art history and a member of the Artists Union, Valentina Alexandrovna is well trained for her function as Memorial's coordinator of creative exhibitions and artists who were victims. But there is something else that links her even more closely to Memorial than the issue of repressed creativity. As the foster daughter of Anton Antonov-Ovseenko, a Soviet diplomat executed in 1938 as an "enemy of the people," she became a victim of the totalitarian system at an early age.

Valentina Alexandrovna had no trouble recalling the moving details of those years. In 1928, when Valentina was five years old, Antonov-Ovseenko came to live with her and her mother, Sofia Ivanovna. Valentina's mother had met him in Czechoslovakia. The three of them spent the following year together in Lithuania, where Antonov-Ovseenko was consul, and the subsequent four years in Warsaw, where he was ambassador. The family returned to Moscow in 1934, where Antonov-Ovseenko at times was summoned to the procurator of the RSFSR. In 1936, when groups of anarchists were active in Spain, he was sent to Barcelona to try to reason with them. Valentina's mother joined him there in the fall of that year.[13] The NKVD probably designed this mission so that they could use his contact with anarchists against him at a later time.

In July 1937, Valentina's parents returned to what she described as an "oppressive" atmosphere in Moscow. Valentina's mother was suffering from heart trouble, so she went to the Crimea to recover, leaving her daughter with Antonov-Ovseenko and a housekeeper to take care of them. Valentina remembers that Antonov-Ovseenko was called to the minister of justice of the RSFSR at the end of September 1937. She also recalled that artists were always coming to visit, so on the night of October 11 when an unfamiliar film director and another man paid a visit to her father (as she considered him), the fourteen-year-old did not find it unusual. The housekeeper had the night off, so Valentina prepared tea for the men and went to her room to go to sleep. She overheard her father talking about his memories of Lenin, apparently for a film they were preparing on "Lenin in October." She recalled that it was noisy in the apartment while she was trying to sleep. Valentina described how she awoke when she heard the door slam shut:

I came out of my room and saw one of the men using the phone in my father's office. He said, "Yes, yes, we're finishing up here." I realized that my father was being taken down the stairs. If I had run I might have caught him, but I just stood there in tears. . . . They didn't even let him say good-bye.

Valentina, at fourteen years of age, did not know what to think; she wondered if all the accusations about "enemy of the people" might have been true. When her mother returned from the Crimea, she too was arrested. After that, Valentina wanted to live with her grandmother but was not allowed to. Instead she was sent to an orphanage at the Danilov Monastery for four years. She recalled, "They took fingerprints and photos of each of us holding a number; somewhere there must be an enormous archive of children's photos." Valentina remembers that she was the only child who did not write to her parents, but she did recollect standing in line at the Butyrka to give fifteen rubles to her parents, though she was never allowed to see them. On February 18, 1938, they were both sentenced to ten years "without the right of correspondence"; "that is," Valentina exclaimed, "a bullet in the back of the head on the day of sentencing." Antonov-Ovseenko and Sofia Ivanovna Antonova-Ovseenko were, indeed, shot that same day in the Lubyanka. Both of Valentina's parents were rehabilitated in 1956. In 1989 she received their death and rehabilitation certificates.

As a fifteen-year-old orphan, Valentina had no way of comprehending the events that were swirling around her. In the ensuing years, she sought enlightenment elsewhere—in the study of art and art history. Half a century later, as a member of Memorial, Valentina is sharing her own experience with others through words and is helping them share their experiences through images that are exhibited nationally and internationally.

Nikita Okhotin, whose primary role in Memorial is connected with the Scientific Research Center and whose Moscow apartment was the initial coordination center for all Memorial-related activities, discussed Memorial's political orientation. He explained that Memorial has no single political platform—some of its members supported the (then) center position of Afanasyev; others, the radical stance of Yevtushenko as well as the views of Yeltsin and Adamovich. "Basically," he summed up, "our policies are those of the Interregional Group,"[14] a liberal opposition faction within the Congress of People's Deputies at that time. Memorial, he asserted, acts as a roof above a number of democracy-seeking organizations. In terms of Memorial's own activism, Okhotin said that only about seventy of the local divisions are active groups. Of these, Moscow has about twenty Memorial activist-strategists, while Leningrad (St. Petersburg) has ten. If every sizable Memorial division had at least a few activists, then we can infer that hundreds of such Memorial members throughout the Soviet Union were striving aggressively for change.[15]

The All-Union (since April 1991 Interrepublic) Memorial has the following organizational structure: at the top is a Social Council of prominent figures who are not active in running the organization but who broaden Memorial's influence by lending their names. The task of decision-making is carried out by a twenty-person work group (*rabochaya kollegiya*), which discusses major questions. The *rabochaya kollegiya* is elected by the Conference (see Appendix B). The Conference also elects Memorial's five co-chairmen. In addition, a 200-person (administrative) Board composed of members from regional Memorial organizations convenes in Moscow twice a year to resolve major issues.[16] Minor issues are resolved by local divisions.

Okhotin discussed some of the problems that Memorial is encountering in trying to help the elderly and the repressed. One of the basic problems was with the Soviet system itself (and its legacy). It has tended to discourage individual initiative and reward passivity. Of the elderly, he confessed, "we don't understand them and they don't understand us."[17] Some do not recognize the scope of Memorial's broad responsibilities to many people. They want Memorial to concentrate on their individual cases and take care of them even though many of the elderly are capable of caring for themselves. "The moral level of the country is low. . . . People have lived in an unfavorable social atmosphere." He explained that because these people have led such difficult lives and suffered so much, they tend to become too dependent on Memorial. But for this kind of support, they do have the option of turning to the "Union of Victims of Repression." This organization within Memorial is primarily in the hands of its youth, who help older people receive material, juridical and medical assistance.

Access to archives, what would be called in America freedom of information, has long been an insurmountable problem in the Soviet Union. Nikita Okhotin, Arseny Roginsky, Yuri Afanasyev and other historians are all too familiar with this. Okhotin discussed the search, collection and analysis of archive materials that will eventually become part of Memorial's Scientific Research Center. For Memorial, appropriate archive material is considered to be anything that provides authentic information about Soviet history, especially unofficial history. The material comes to Memorial via the reception room or simply by mail—poems, notes, memoirs, declarations of support for Memorial, information, photographs, letters from camps, questions about relatives. Okhotin considers every letter to be testimony. Memorial receives 500–2,000 letters per month, 80 to 90% of which deal with repressions. Many of those are from released victims of psychiatric repression. About ten letters a month are from Stalinists.

Another principal source of Memorial's information comes from recording oral histories. In cases in which the subject has difficulty ambulating or writing, the oral history group joins forces with the Russian State University of the Humanities' (formerly Historical Archive Institute's) Oral History Laboratory and goes to them to record interviews on tape. In its initial days, Memorial was faced with an oral historian's nightmare. Interviewers often had to transcribe tapes and re-use them, because cassette tapes are one of the numberless "deficit" commodities. Now they are trying to transfer interviews to reel-to-reel tapes. Ten members of Memorial conduct about two hundred interviews per year.[18]

The June 1989 oral history expedition to the Kuban led by Darya Khubova has already been mentioned in Chapter 6. O. V. Moiseyev led another such expedition to the province of Pskov in July 1989 to study repression in churches and religious awareness through interviews.[19] Ongoing oral history research missions investigate themes such as "Childhood in the USSR," "The Repressed Church and Contemporary Religious Consciousness," "Popular Opposition to Bolshevism" and "The Deportation of Small Soviet Nationalities (1943–44)." One can consult the relevant archives to gather facts on the popular opposition to Bolshevism but find little of value, explained Memorial's chief oral historian, Darya Khubova.[20] For meaningful information, it is necessary to travel to places like the Urals, Siberia and Altai where the revolts took place and interview the people who remember them. It is critical to carry out research on such themes while there are still eye-witnesses. One observation made by the team of historians is that different groups of people processed and recollected the same experience (for example, deportation) in different ways. How the oral memoirs can differ became apparent when the oral history group was trying to reconstruct events attendant to the deportation of the Crimean Tatars, Cossacks, Kabardins and Balkars. The deported Muslims emphasized in their recollection the route and the journey from the Crimea to Siberia, while the Cossacks selectively remembered the artificial famine.[21]

One hopes that a new project entitled "Resistance to Totalitarianism in Eastern Europe: June 1953—Berlin, November 1956—Budapest, August 1968—Prague" will fill in the considerable blank spots left by archives like the GRU (State Intelligence Administration). The GRU has been sealed for fifty years to protect the privacy of those involved who are still alive.[22] The project's aim is to gather interviews from soldiers who were stationed in the area, local civilians who were unaware of the situation, and witnesses at the scenes where these events took place. Indeed, for this particular subject, laden as it is with deep historical and political conflicts, an oral history is the only source of information.[23]

However, documenting oral history has other uses besides establishing the validity of historical events. It can also be employed to infer the cultural definitions of a society, its weltanschauung. The project "The Russian Intelligentsia and the Problems of Personal Culture" examines the internal and external manifestations of social class and culture. "The state imposed biographies on people," explained Darya Khubova. Many members of the intelligentsia were simply given a new sociocultural status by the state. Khubova gave the example of an illiterate cleaning woman whose mannerisms and demeanor did not seem to fit such a job. An interview with her revealed that her mother had been an aristrocrat and her father a White general. In other circumstances, this woman would have remained a member of the intelligentsia. Her charismatic bearing as a member of a higher social class was apparent to the insightful observer.[24] In contrast to those who remained under repression, members of the intelligentsia who emigrated were able to preserve their cultural status. The oral history group is attempting to determine both how these groups of people see themselves and whether they consider themselves as the "intelligentsia." A similar project will compare the culture of the Soviet Jewish community who stayed with those who emigrated. These are methodologically complex issues. It takes many visits, hours of interviews on audiocassettes, and sometimes videotaping to make an accurate assessment of the subject. Each project involves about twenty-five interviews. At some point, there will be an audiocassette archive to facilitate scholarly analysis of collected materials and films from the oral history expeditions.

Another method of collecting information is field work gathered by research expeditions.[25] In May 1989 Arseny Roginsky led a fifteen-person expedition to the Solovetsky islands to study the history, topography and buildings of the camps and to work with scholars from Leningrad and Arkhangelsk on a seminar on the topic. During that same year Alexander Vologodsky, a molecular biologist and coordinator of photography and the photo archive of Memorial, led a seven-person mission along 120 kilometers of the railroad from Salekhard to Igarka. Photos and videos were made of the twenty camps visited and presented to the public. They titled the presentation, "The History of the Construction of the 'Dead Road.' "

All this information, Nikita Okhotin explained, will eventually go into an archive, which the Scientific Research Center wants to be not simply a collection but a data bank, an "electronic archive" of materials on repression. By February 1990, it exceeded 10,000 units.[26] Memorial workers are constantly occupied with systematizing and copying the archive. In 1992 an agreement was made between Memorial and the International Institute of Social History in Amsterdam to copy Memorial's (already) 30,000-unit archive onto microfiche. These films are to be available for research at the Amsterdam institute.[27]

A card catalog of victims of repression is also being prepared. The Memorial archive aspires to include over 1,000 books and hundreds of newspaper articles as well as copies of materials from state archives. The library and museum sections of the Scientific Research Center house this growing collection as well as journals, reference books, materials of Party congresses and conferences and books that were banned from state libraries.

Okhotin explained that Memorial's Scientific Research Center strives for the speedy release of publications in informative journals and exhibitions rather than concentrating on making films or publishing books, which cost a considerable amount of time and money. The subjects covered indicate Memorial's broad range of interest. It published the first volume of a historical almanac called *Links* ("Svenya") in 1991. It is a collection of articles by Memorial historians on such topics as "Power, People, Culture," "In the Struggle for a Political Regime," "Map of the Gulag," "Henchmen and Victims." Additionally, an annotated bibliography, *Repression in the USSR: 1918–1984*, is being compiled. Ongoing research topics include "repressed science," "history of the bourgeois and socialist parties after October" and "the general history of the Gulag."[28]

A number of exhibitions can also be credited to Memorial. Those that have been completed or are being prepared focus on themes such as "Monuments to Victims of Stalinist Repression," "A Friendship Cemented in Blood, Germany-USSR: 1939–1941, Hitler-Stalin Pact," "The Country as a Gulag, the Gulag as a Country." ("Where do you draw the border?" asks Okhotin.[29]) "Repressed Childhood," "The Fate of Soviet Women," "Famine and Dekulakization" and "Art of the Camps" are other exhibition themes. "Art of the Camps," organized by Memorial and Artist Union member Valentina Alexandrovna Tikhanova, contains mostly portraits and self-portraits on notebook paper or plywood, done by imprisoned artists often with pencil stubs.[30] Lev Razgon commented on this exhibition: "If an album of these drawings were published without captions or any references to where they were made it would still be clear who these people are and why their faces carry the stigma of upcoming death."[31] In 1989 alone, Memorial collected 35,000 rubles at exhibitions. Most of the money went to provide material help for former prisoners of Stalinist camps.

In July 1990, Nikita Okhotin, Arseny Roginsky and Nikita Petrov officially registered the Scientific Information and Research Center (NITS) of Memorial. The center is now an independent entity within Memorial. It works in cooperation with local Memorial divisions and other similarly oriented national and international scientific and educational organizations. Memorial also has an active human rights center headed by Dmitry Leonov. This division of Memorial monitors human rights violations throughout the former Soviet Union. Gradually, over time, all the major Memorial divisions have been registered. To the 1990 issue of the lack of registration of the All-Union Memorial, Okhotin, after enumerating and describing the previously mentioned activities, triumphantly asserted, "We are doing fine without (All-Union) registration."[32]

The fact that each local Memorial has its own way of operating became apparent when I visited Veniamin Iofe, one of the Leningrad Memorial's co-chairmen, and Tatyana Pritykina, one of its founding members. Their division has over seven hundred members. As was the case in Moscow, Memorial archives were stored in private apartments. Iofe, who joined Memorial in the fall of 1988 and works in its historical archive section, had the card catalog of all archival material in two mobile suitcases in his home. For all of Memorial's widespread popularity, the safety of the archives was still thought to depend on the speed with which they could be moved and hidden. The cards contain biographical material on victims, camp memoirs, photographs and letters. Iofe explained how material on the various subjects is distributed among apartments. These subjects include: Stalin's repressions; later, post-Stalin repressions; repression from 1968 to 1985; a new folder from 1985 onward; deported populations; workers sent to the Soviet Union from territories occupied by the Germans; inmates of German camps sent to Soviet camps; material on the Solovetsky islands.[33] Leningrad (St. Petersburg) Memorial members have organizational meetings one evening a week, and once a week a reception room to which victims can come is open at a local museum.

In Leningrad, attention is directed to the plight of Tsarist as well as early and later Soviet political prisoners. Iofe commented that the Leningrad Memorial would like to locate the monument to victims of repression in Revolution Square (this eventually happened) and rename the square "Revolution Victim Square." It is appropriately located across from the Petro-Pavlovsk fortress, a prison for political prisoners in Tsarist times. In this spirit the Leningrad City Council promised to provide two rooms for Memorial in the "House of Former Political Prisoners and Exiles," built during Tsarist times. Upstairs, the nineteen apartments had been inhabited by Mensheviks, Socialist Revolutionaries (SRs), and later victims of the revolution; downstairs, a club, meeting hall and library were housed. Iofe believes that this place, previously inhabited by creators of the revolution who subsequently became its victims, is a fitting center for the Leningrad Memorial.

Though Memorial promoted candidates for the Leningrad Council, Iofe emphasized that it cannot be called a political party because it has no single position. It unites people from various sides, from the Right to the Left, "because," Iofe reasoned, "everyone was repressed."[34] Although Memorial does not have a single political position, it does have a narrow political range. This narrow political range includes: support of legally based governance, checks and balances on power, the defense of individual, human and legal rights. The limited funds at the organization's disposal are spent for education-oriented activities and social welfare programs such as subsidized medical treatment, rent and free transport. Iofe discussed the 1981 compensation law. He presented it as a cynical and ludicrous example of "progress" toward gaining victims' rights: "A decree was made stating that anyone unlawfully imprisoned before 1981 who has been rehabilitated is entitled to receive lost wages for the whole term, but not for more than two months!"[35] Leningrad's Memorial is also trying to resolve this and other instances of legalistic legerdemain related to restitution for victims.

The Leningrad Memorial has published a number of issues of *Vestnik*, to which its co-chairman Iofe has contributed articles on themes such as the necessity to "know every fate" and the Solovetsky monastery's unholy transformation. What started as "one of the Russian Orthodox spiritual centers became, after 1923, a symbol of the Gulag Archipelago."[36] *Vestnik* published a letter by Iofe requesting the chairman of the Solovetsky regional executive committee to allow services to be conducted at the graves of victims of mass repression on the Solovetsky islands (a group of six islands in the White Sea in the Arkhangelsk province of Russia). The request was granted.

The editor-in-chief of *Vestnik*, Tatyana Pritykina of the Leningrad Cultural Foundation, discussed the Leningrad Memorial's strong cultural-historical orientation and its unique history of close ties with an established organization. Academician Likhachev, a prisoner on Solovki (the Solovetsky islands) when he was young, is both the chairman of the Leningrad Cultural Foundation and a member of Memorial's Social Council. In 1988, Tatyana Pritykina explained, the foundation became a central meeting place for "stormy discussions" of the newly emerging informal groups.[37] It was also the Cultural Foundation that announced the Memorial monument competition for that city and helped in the conducting of exhibitions. In Leningrad, as in Moscow, there was a strong effort to understate Memorial's political orientation by emphasizing its cultural, educational, historical and social work. This was quite understandable in a country like the Soviet Union, where the term "political organization" immediately circumscribed options.

This apolitical policy has been voiced by many. Historian Arseny Roginsky was outspoken in his assertion that Memorial was not a political organization. Considering his history, he had reason to be wary of the political label. He talked about how Memorial gets criticized from both sides of the spectrum of public opinion. Some see Memorial as a purely political organization and criticize it for including the Lenin period in its investigation of repression. Others accuse Memorial of being afraid to study the terror of the Lenin period and that of the 1960s, 1970s and 1980s. Roginsky maintained, "We are studying history, where artificial borders can never be placed. Repressions started before Stalin and there were political prisoners under Khrushchev, Brezhnev, Andropov, etc."[38] He recalled that two years earlier (in 1988) the psychological barriers to public understanding were much greater, but gradually people are changing their way of thinking about the past and present.

Roginsky feels that people can only be convinced by evidence.[39] Memorial believes that when repression continues, action is called for. Sergei Kuznetsov, an "uncompromising"[40] dissident and member of the Democratic Union, was arrested in 1989 for distributing flyers detailing corruption in the police and KGB. He was charged with "slandering officials." For two months thereafter, Memorial led a daily picket line in front of the office of the procurator of the Soviet Union. Despite the political activism exhibited, Roginsky maintained that the issue was human rights and not political. He stressed that the basic values of culture, morality and law are the fundamentals upon which to build, because they will ultimately have a greater impact on society than would a direct partisan political struggle.[41]

Whether Memorial or its commentators label the organization (during the Soviet era) "political" is, perhaps, irrelevant. In a country as highly politicized as the Soviet Union, the issues that Memorial addressed and demanded response to had an inescapable political cast. Even something as seemingly neutral as history is political. History is always *someone's* story. The Soviet state has, for decades, ensured that its version of history was the only history extant. To ensure this uniformity of opinion, the state employed such widely recognized historical critics as censors, prisons, labor camps and psychiatric hospitals. That is the politics of history; in the Soviet Union, it is also the history of politics.

This chapter has explored Memorial from the inside, recording the perspectives of many who are directing the organization along its still incompletely charted course. The issues of political activity and political partisanship have always been debatable. Also uncertain is the degree of popular and official resistance to Memorial's expanding humanism. The next and concluding chapter will examine the political activities of Memorial as well as the resistance to its efforts.

NOTES

1. *Vedomosti Memoriala* (Moscow), 28 January 1989; *Informatsiony Byulleten* (Moscow) 11, 1990; *Sodeistviye, Press-Byulleten Tambovskogo Memoriala* (Tambov) 11 (August), 12 (September), 14 (November), 1989; *Letopis Terrora* (Tomsk), April-June 1989; *Vestnik Leningradskogo Obshchestva "Memorial"* (Leningrad), May-August 1989; *Svoboda, Gazeta Press-Tsentra Moskovskogo Memoriala* (Moscow) 1, March 1990; *Kuzbasskiye Vedomosti* (Kuzbassk) 3, March 1990; *Kotlovan, Khibinskogo Obshchestva "Memorial"* (Khibinsk), March, September, October 1990.

2. Vera Ivanovna, interview held at Memorial's reception area, Chernyakovsky 2, Moscow, April 10, 1990.

3. Galina Moiseyevna, interview held at Chernyakovsky 2, Moscow, April 21, 1990.

4. Anna Kasatika, interview held at Chernyakovsky 2, Moscow, April 21, 1990.

5. Nikita Okhotin, interview held at his Moscow home, April 9, 1990.

6. Olga Cherepova, interview held at Chernyakovsky 2, Moscow, April 21, 1990.

7. Arseny Roginsky, interview held at Historical Archive Institute, Moscow, April 20, 1990.

8. Olga Cherepova, interview, April 21, 1990.

9. Eva-Maria Stege, personal letter, Berlin, November 1989.

10. Olga Cherepova, interview, April 21, 1990.

11. Nikita Okhotin, interview, April 9, 1990.

12. Suzanna Solomonovna Pechuro, interview held at her Moscow home, April 13, 1990. Subsequent quotes are also from this interview.

13. Valentina Alexandrovna Tikhanova, interview held at her Moscow home, April 23, 1990. Subsequent quotes are also from this interview.

14. Nikita Okhotin, interview, April 9, 1990.

15. Nikita Petrov, interview held at Second World Center, Amsterdam, October 1990.

16. Vladimir Pribylovsky, *Slovar Novykh Politicheskykh Partii i Organizatii Rossii* (*Dictionary of New Political Parties and Organizations in Russia*), Information Group "Panorama," Moscow, November 1991, p. 40.

17. Nikita Okhotin, interview, April 9, 1990. Subsequent quote and information are also from this interview.

18. Ibid.

19. N. G. Okhotin, A. B. Roginsky, "Project Electronic Archive," otchyot za 1989 (report of activities), Moscow, February 4, 1990.

20. Darya Khubova, interview held in the Oral History Laboratory of the Russian State University of the Humanities in Moscow, April 22, 1992.

21. Ibid.

22. Ibid.

23. Ibid.

24. Ibid.

25. Okhotin and Roginsky, "Project electronic archive."

26. Nikita Okhotin, interview, April 9, 1990.

27. *Bulletin of Central and East-European Activities* (International Institute of Social History) (February 1992): 2.

28. Nikita Okhotin, interview, April 9, 1990.

29. Ibid.

30. *New Times* (Moscow) 27, 1990.

31. Ibid.

32. Nikita Okhotin, interview, April 9, 1990.

33. Veniamin Iofe, interview held at his Leningrad home, April 17, 1990.

34. Ibid.

35. Ibid.

36. *Vestnik* (Leningrad Memorial Society) 3, Leningrad, June 1989.

37. Tatyana Pritykina, interview held at Leningrad Cultural Foundation, Leningrad, April 16, 1990.

38. Arseny Roginsky, interview, April 20, 1990.

39. Ibid.

40. Oleg Orlov, interview held at his Moscow home, April 11, 1990.

41. Arseny Roginsky, interview, April 20, 1990.

CHAPTER 8 _____

The Politics of Memorial

Thus far we have been recounting three overlapping histories—the period under Stalin, the larger period with which Memorial is occupied and the history of Memorial itself. The dividing line between historical investigation and political exposé is a fine one. It may depend on whether the people and events under scrutiny are dead or alive. Studying the Tsar is history; studying Gorbachev is history and politics. In between is the study of Lenin and Stalin. Are they indeed dead or, as Memorial fears, still very much alive and very political? Regardless of anyone's wish that Memorial hew to a narrow definition of historical enlightenment, it has little choice but to be active on behalf of its growing constituency. It must do so for at least two reasons: the first is to stay alive in the face of active opposition; the second is to fulfill its humanistic promise.

During March and April 1990, campaign leaflets and posters from Memorial and Democratic Russia could be found all over the Tagansky district of Moscow, endorsing Alexander Vologodsky, the "democratic" candidate and Memorial photography coordinator, as district representative to the Moscow City Council. One of these, on a Memorial letterhead, stated: "by voting for the candidate supported by MEMORIAL, you are voting for: legally based government, political and economic freedom, civil peace . . . and freedom of word, religion, and political party."[1] It was signed by Adamovich and Afanasyev as People's Deputies and leading figures in Memorial. Another such endorsement from the bloc known as Democratic Russia was signed by Gavriil Popov, then mayor of Moscow. Technically, Memorial was not allowed to nominate candidates (as was

illustrated with Andrei Sakharov's candidacy for People's Deputy), because they did not have official registration.[2] Their candidates, therefore,
made up part of the bloc, Democratic Russia. Memorial encouraged voters
to support the platform of this political grouping. Well aware of the
people's sense of impending civil war, Vologodsky asserted that democracy and a healthy market economy were the only means to peacefully
lead the country out of crisis. He added that local soviets (councils) should
be in charge of their own territories. How ironic that the revolutionary
concept of power to the Soviets remained still unrealized. More than
seventy years since the Bolshevik battle cry "All Power to the Soviets!"
galvanized the nation, a different group with a different history is trying
to bring the nation into a system by which the checks and balances on
power will be institutionalized, a system the Bolsheviks never intended to
create. The molecular biologist and photographer-turned-politician, Alexander Vologodsky, remarked, "Memorial stands for an anti-totalitarian
state," and "it is a rather political organization."[3]

Oleg Orlov, an ardent political spokesman in Memorial and 1990
co-chairman of its Moscow chapter, discussed the organization's political
development. In 1988, as Memorial was beginning to take shape, other
organizations were also forming. When the Moscow People's Front, an
emerging political movement unifying opposition groups, was created in
that year, Memorial joined it in the capacity of an organizational committee. But after one of their first meetings in Pushkin Square was broken up
by police, Memorial formally left the organization, though the two continued to work together. Up to that point, Memorial had only been an
initiative group, but after leaving the People's Front it became a movement
unto itself.[4] When events involved democratic reformist issues such as the
defense of Yeltsin, upcoming elections, violence in Tbilisi and Baku,
Lithuanian independence, Article 6 of the Constitution, and the like,
Memorial activists reached out to the public in two ways—through signature campaigns and open meetings. Observers were also sent to Baku,
where, as a result of pogroms and military action against civilians, an
estimated 250 people died. Memorial collected evidence by conducting a
survey in hospitals. These testimonies were then turned over to People's
Deputies.[5]

The status of Lithuania was another politically contentious topic with
which Memorial was occupied. A meeting of the work group of the
Moscow Memorial voiced full support for Lithuanian independence.[6]
Additionally, Memorial members worked with the Moscow Helsinki
Group, maintaining a list of political prisoners in the Soviet Union for
presentation to the procurator of the Soviet Union.[7] Their goal was the

creation of a group that would work in cooperation with independent human rights organizations to review political cases.

The draft resolutions made at an All-Union Memorial conference in June 1990 are undeniably political in tone and aspiration. They include demands to the government to abolish economic sanctions against Lithuania and to begin negotiations on the basis of Lithuania's March 11 declaration of independence. Additionally, they call for political parties and social organizations to unite all democratic forces in the nation on this issue, committing the leadership of Memorial to make the necessary contacts to start the process. Even more forthright as a statement of political activism is Resolution 2:

Memorial as an organization, placing the goals for itself of the destruction of the basis of totalitarian power and the transition to a legal government, cannot stand outside the realm of political life. However, [regarding this] Memorial does not exclusively support any single political doctrine and thus cannot be a collective member of any one political party to the extent that it unites people on the basis of fundamental humanitarian values . . . [and] human rights, people of different political views, who are trying to realize various, even opposite political economic, social and national projects.[8]

This may be true, but one does not have to be a part of any particular political party to be recognized as belonging to a politically oriented organization, all the more so when that organization asks nothing less than changing the very structure of the state as well as the state's relationship to the people.

Some of the various forms of opposition that Memorial has faced have already been discussed. They range from the state's reluctance to condemn the crimes and criminals of the past, to bedrock individuals like Ivan Shekhovtsev who defended Stalin's honor in court seventeen times. In Georgia, Stalin's birthplace, an international association with a following of 1,513 members (in early 1990) was established in his honor. It was headed by Lieutenant General Irakli Dzhordzhadze, who had trained in officers' school with Stalin's son, Jacob.[9] Although the Ivan Shekhovtsevs and General Irakli Dzhordzhadzes do not in themselves represent any substantial opposition, they do indicate the presence of arch-conservative sentiments that, given an economic crisis, could present a real source of danger. In November 1990, statues of Stalin could still be found in Georgia, even a full-length one in his home town of Gori. A journalist surveying this phenomenon recorded local sentiments on Stalin. He relates those of a "sweet little old lady" who reads the Bible daily:

When Stalin lived, there were no robberies, no thieves breaking into your
home. . . . The persecution of the church? No, no. That wasn't Stalin. That was
Lenin. The executions? No, no. That wasn't Stalin. That was Molotov. Molotov
signed the execution papers. . . . When Stalin was in power, potatoes were 15
kopeks a kilo. Today they are two rubles.[10]

Then there were the Party conservatives who, afraid of the competition
from an independent organization, successfully delayed Memorial's process of registration. By 1991, the government had neither registered the
All-Union Society nor made relevant files in the Institute of Marxism and
Leninism and KGB archives accessible. This served as a potential source
of hope for defendants of the old order, at least to the extent that it indicated
that their opponents were not enjoying full support.[11]

Memorial encounters additional sources of resistance from Russian
nationalists, a large group who feel that Memorial places all the blame on
Stalin and his associates while sparing other communists. Some sections
of the Right publish essays in such literary journals as *Moskva*, *Molodaya
Gvardia* and *Nash Sovremennik* to express their anti-Memorial sentiments.
With titles such as "A Memorial to Whom?" they accuse Memorial of
selective rehabilitation and sensationalism and assert that the Terror began
before Stalin[12] (Memorial does not deny the latter premise). In some cases,
anti-Memorial literature, voicing the views of the extreme Right, argues
in favor of some of Stalin's purges.[13] Russian nationalists whose ideals go
back to the pre-Soviet period, the Russian Orthodox church, the pre-col-
lectivization village and a deeply ingrained anti-Semitism, often find
Stalin a "lesser evil" than Lenin, Trotsky, Bukharin and Zinoviev.[14] After
all, they reason, Stalin eliminated growing internationalist elements, made
Russia a world power and led it in the victorious Great Patriotic War[15]
(during which time, significantly, his propaganda efforts evoked images
of great *Russian* warriors). The neo-Stalinists represent a variation on this
theme. They do not consider Stalin a lesser evil, but rather a great Soviet
leader, and they express their longing for the state of order that the country
enjoyed under him. According to Arseny Roginsky, such xenophobic
groupings consider Europeanites, Freemasons, Jews and Memorial to be
one and the same. At present, Roginsky believes, Memorial is stronger
than the forces opposing it. But with reference to Pamyat and similar
organizations, he added, "these are our future enemies, not today's."[16]

What can be done to ensure that Stalinist forces will not rise again?
Some suggest a Nuremberg tribunal-style legal condemnation of the
crimes of Stalinism by bringing the responsible individuals to trial. They
assert that by establishing such legal precedents, de-Stalinization would

become irreversible.[17] They point out that, in theory, if posthumous rehabilitations are possible, so too are posthumous prosecutions, and justice could still be applied to those henchmen who are still alive. But prominent anti-Stalinists like Andrei Sakharov and Yelena Bonner considered the moral recovery of the Soviet people to be more important than revenge and the question of guilt, with so many involved, too complicated. Thus, they argued that the mass repression must be declared illegal, but that further action should be taken in the spirit of humanism and charity.[18] Alternatively, in a letter to the editor that appeared in the periodical *Commentary* under the headline "Crime But No Punishment," Zbigniew Brzezinski expressed his anger at the fact that no "Stalinist murderer" has been punished for his crimes.[19] Furthermore, thousands of them still don their medals at revolutionary celebrations, and people like Serepenko, the "Eichmann" of the Katyn massacre, live in comfort. The issue that a trial would resolve, Brzezinski argued, is that the criminality of the NKVD-KGB and the Party would be acknowledged.[20] Given the uncertainty of such a trial's outcome and effect, it would seem that democratic institutions are the only true safeguard for preventing the re-emergence of Stalinist elements. But attaining such a state is especially difficult considering the total lack of any democratic tradition in Russia.

The trial issue became exacerbated after the collapse of the Soviet Union. On July 7, 1992, a hearing regarding the activities of the Communist Party, to which we already referred in Chapter 3, was instigated. President Yeltsin asserted that the hearing could determine "Russia's destiny."[21] It attracted both old communists defending the system and democrats representing the victims of that same system. Gleb Yakunin, a dissident Russian Orthodox priest, hoped that it would eventually lead to juridical condemnation of the Party for "crimes against humanity."[22] Alexander Yakovlev, a constitutional scholar from the Russian Academy of Sciences' Institute of State and Law, put it into a historical context, pointing out that whatever the outcome, if the trial is based on law, "it will be valuable, showing we are building a rule of law state."[23]

A number of economic, political and cultural factors will be consequential for Memorial and for the New Independent States (NIS) at large. Of considerable importance is the amount of Western contact and support. Memorial has been aided (Russian nationalists would say abetted) in its uphill struggle by various organizations in the West that have provided money, technical equipment, travel abroad for Memorial members to observe Western methods and consult archives, exchange programs and, most important, general moral support. These Western contributors will be briefly acknowledged here.

The Ford Foundation of New York has provided significant grants, money that Memorial uses for publications and the development of its organization. These are administered by the "Friends of Memorial" society. The Soros Foundation, also based in New York, has donated essential technical apparatus for Memorial, including computers for storing archival information and cassette tape recorders for gathering oral histories.

Other organizations have furnished more specific kinds of help. Radio Liberty/Radio Free Europe has contributed a copy of its samizdat collection to aid in Memorial's research on dissidence. The Second World Center, based in Amsterdam, has provided Memorial with material support (technical equipment), needed history books and intern exchange programs. It also cooperated with Memorial and the International Institute of Social History to create the exhibition, "Beyond the Friendship of the Peoples: Nationalism and Anti-Semitism at the End of the Soviet Era," a phenomenon with which the world has become painfully familiar in recent years.

The Heinrich Böll Stiftung invited Memorial members to its base in Bonn for history workshops on, among other subjects, oral history, the methodological and political problems of "history from below" in the Soviet Union and (former) West Germany and workers deported to the Soviet Union from German-occupied territories. Further plans were laid for the continuation of such workshops.[24]

The Friends of Memorial association has been formed in the United States under the aegis of Columbia University's Harriman Institute. This society is made up of emigré and Western scholars as well as others who are involved in Soviet affairs and who share common goals focusing on cooperation, scholarship and research. It facilitates the exchange of information (by mutual visits), assistance in the collection and processing of data, the compilation of a single database, help in creating a library and bibliography of literature on Soviet political repression and the publication of a Russian-English reference journal on Stalinism. Joint exhibitions shown in the United States and the NIS also make up part of the Friends of Memorial agenda.[25]

One extensive Memorial project on the Soviet dissident movement from the 1950s to the 1980s concluded in a Ford Foundation–sponsored conference in Moscow in 1992 (see Epilogue). Ongoing cooperation with all these organizations can effectively expand the scope of Memorial and help assure Memorial's unhindered development.

But the degree of hindrance to Memorial's work and, indeed, the fate of Memorial are inextricably linked to the fate of the NIS as a whole and the political course it follows. Many of the initial demands voiced by Memorial, like the construction of the monument and the restitution of Solzhenitsyn's citizenship, have gradually been granted. In fact, Solzhenitsyn has even been made an honorary citizen of Ryazan, where he wrote his most renowned works.[26] Other issues, though, are still far from settled. The question raised in Chapter 1 on the scope of the Terror, despite the investigations, remains unanswered. Alexander Krushelnitsky, a historian and instructor at Moscow's Russian State University of the Humanities, explained that without proper access to official archives, oral history is the only way to supplement the incomplete figures available.[27] At an October 1990 meeting in Moscow of the All-Union Memorial Board, Lev Razgon discussed the problem of not having the official statistics about those who were arrested and executed as well as those who died in prisons and camps. The irony, he pointed out, is that "these numbers exist, they are in a certain place not far from here, on Dzerzhinsky Square. But we do not have these numbers. And we will not know our past until these precise numbers are officially published."[28] Even in 1992 many of the files regarding the fate of victims of Stalinism remained inaccessible,[29] and others had simply been destroyed. But even if we could discover the official story, even if all the names and numbers could be published, many questions would still be unanswered, because there is always a difference between official description ("the top down") and "the way things really happened" ("the bottom up") view of history. Especially in totalitarian (or recently dissolved totalitarian) regimes, oral history provides a necessary corrective to the official story. Darya Khubova aptly points out that Memorial's goal of enlightenment is in itself political, for what is enlightenment but the desire to change people's way of thinking? And, indeed, there may be people who want to prevent such a change from occurring.[30] Although the movement toward greater freedom is succeeding, the gains are vulnerable to reversal if political instability undermines democracy.

Future historians chronicling the political history of the Soviet Union and its aftermath will be better able to assess Memorial's contribution to its then-existing forms of government. What they will describe is an organization devoted to enlightening a wary populace, many of whom preferred to remain unenlightened; an organization that persistently fought official and non-official resistance because of the proscribed issues it pursued. They will describe an organization that, nevertheless, managed to place a monument to victims of totalitarianism right in front of the KGB, the shrine of totalitarianism. Future schoolchildren may wonder why obtaining official registration and official statistics were such insurmountable obstacles for a "historical society." They will learn that even pursuit of the historical truth in the Soviet Union of the late 1980s and early 1990s was a direct threat to the authorities, the authors of official history. What they will see, in any case, is that despite the absence of official support, Memorial was still able to reconstruct a picture of the Soviet past, examine the pathology of Stalinism and return the power of knowledge to the people.

NOTES

1. Memorial campaign leaflet (Moscow), April 1990.

2. Oleg Orlov, interview held at his Moscow home, April 11, 1990.

3. Alexander Vologodsky, interview held at his Moscow home, April 15 and 22, 1990.

4. Oleg Orlov, interview, April 11, 1990.

5. Ibid.

6. *Informatsiony Byulleten* (Moscow), 23 March 1990.

7. Oleg Orlov, interview, April 11, 1990.

8. "Rezolutii Konferentii Obshchestva 'Memorial'," draft resolutions (Moscow), 1–3 June 1990.

9. Walter Laqueur, *Stalin: The Glasnost Revelations* (New York: Charles Scribner's Sons, 1990), p. 272.

10. *International Herald Tribune*, 1 November 1990.

11. Laqueur, pp. 271–272.

12. Ibid.

13. Ibid., p. 274.

14. Ibid.

15. Ibid, pp. 274–275.

16. Arseny Roginsky, interview held at Historical Archive Institute, Moscow, April 20, 1990.

17. Laqueur, p. 264.

18. Ibid.

19. *Commentary* (New York) 6, December 1990.

20. Ibid.

21. *International Herald Tribune*, 8 July 1992.

22. Ibid.

23. Ibid.

24. *Memorial, Aufklärung der Geschichte und Gestaltung der Zukunft* (Bonn: Heinrich Böll Stiftung, e.V., November 1989).

25. Mark von Hagen, Project for Friends of Memorial, New York.

26. *International Herald Tribune*, 27 November 1990.

27. Alexander Krushelnitsky, interview held at Second World Center in Amsterdam, December 7, 1990.

28. *Kotlovan*, Spetsialny Vypusk Khibinskogo otdeleniya obshchestva "Memorial" (Special newspaper edition from the Khibinsk section of Memorial), Fall, 1990.

29. Vera Tolz, "Access to KGB and CPSU Archives in Russia," *RFERL Research Report* 1, no. 16 (17 April 1992): 1–7.

30. Darya Khubova, interview held at Second World Center in Amsterdam, January 25, 1991.

Epilogue: "Today We Are Historians of Dissidence, and Not Dissidents"

In August 1992, one year after the "three days that shook the world," Memorial hosted an unprecedented international conference in Moscow. Its importance lay only partly in the informed, experiential, scientific presentations of its distinguished participants who gathered to discuss the dissident movement from the 1950s to the 1980s. The conference's larger significance derived from its very being, from the fact that it occurred at all, a fact validated by this convocation. As a historical society (with a barely hidden agenda), Memorial had triumphed first by enduring, next by prevailing,[1] and finally by celebrating its historicity by self-reflection.

Ironically and appropriately, the gathering was held on the grounds of the former higher Communist Party school. The Russian State University of the Humanities (RGGU) has become the new occupant of its campus. The location provided other telling ironies. Both on November 7, 1991 (Revolution Day), and on April 22, 1992 (Lenin's birthday), flowers had been laid at one of the last remaining busts of Lenin. In August 1992, only the flowers remained at that site—Lenin had been replaced by a garden! The long, sparsely lit corridors of the dormitory, which used to be trodden by privileged foreign communists who came to the capital to brush up on their studies of Marx and Engels, are now occupied by national and international students, guests of Memorial and visiting scholars.

Memorial's power to choose the time, the place, and the people for this conference reflects a major change in its status since its first international conference on oral history held in 1989 (see Chapter 6). In the fall of 1991, the Interrepublic Memorial received official registration at the RSFSR

Ministry of Justice.[2] Its official registration enabled Memorial to invite foreign guests whose visas did not depend on special favors from embassy friends. The guests included representatives from Amnesty International (London), the Ford Foundation (New York), Radio Liberty/Radio Free Europe (Munich), the Second World Center (Amsterdam) and Western universities.

But success has its own problems, welcome but problematic nevertheless. Prominent among those addressed by the participants were the issues of identifying, redefining and characterizing the dissident movement as well as the present and future role of Memorial. With regard to identity, the dissidents knew who they were, but if the label was to be extended to other people and other movements, it would be necessary to define just what they were. With regard to their function in the still-evolving post-Soviet political climate, there was a consensus that the new freedoms could be taken as granted but could not be taken as established and would require continued monitoring.

The twin themes—"what are we and how can our future be true to our past"—were appropriately embodied in the choice of Alexander Daniel as conference chairman. The Memorial scientific council member is the son of Yuli Daniel, who, together with Andrei Sinyavsky, symbolized the beginning of the Soviet dissident era with their satirical critiques on the absurdities of Soviet life and their subsequent persecution and trial in 1966. Sinyavsky and Daniel had carried the coffin of Pasternak; they also carried forward the literary nonconformist tradition. Their fate was one of the early indications that Brezhnev's policies had turned away from the "thaw" toward repression. The generation of Yuli Daniel's son is successor to those who tried to break down totalitarian structures. They accept it as their task to move democracy forward.

Alexander Daniel attempted to circumscribe the issue of identity by challenging the audience with these questions: Who can we consider a dissident? Who is not—and why? What are dissident activities? What was the dissident movement? For example, should groups like ethnic Germans and Crimean Tatars be considered dissidents on account of official efforts to suppress their ethnic identity?

Along with looking inward as part of its search for identity, Memorial was looking backward in an effort to establish the origins of the dissident movement. Daniel pointed out that samizdat (unofficial press, publications and literature) began appearing in 1961. This information grapevine to correct official lies, a new cultural phenomenon, ushered in the social movement of the next seven years. During the subsequent four years (1969–1973), as a result of continued repression, the movement became politicized, and in turn the political sphere began to encompass human rights issues.

Eventually, this political activism took the form of a historical investigation of the repressors and the repressed. By 1992, the latter group was no longer enveloped in the totalitarian system. Daniel's words, "Today we are historians of dissidence, and not dissidents," best reflected that the time had come to undertake a historical investigation of the dissident movement itself. Still missing are important details regarding the people, processes and events that bridged the period between Sinyavsky and Daniel and the present dissident movement.

Peter Reddaway is a pioneer in the field of study of totalitarian subversion of science and, more particularly, of the political abuse of Soviet psychiatry. He reviewed some of the history of the struggle to inform international psychiatric organizations of the flagrant medical and ethical violations practiced by the All-Union Society of Psychiatrists. Among such practices was the use of the ad hoc diagnosis of "sluggish schizophrenia" to incarcerate dissidents in psychiatric hospitals. This was belatedly discovered or reluctantly recognized through unofficial Soviet and foreign networks, victimized families, doctors and forensic reports. A prominent example was the "case history" of General Pyotr Grigorenko, a decorated war hero who became a human rights advocate. In consequence of this advocacy, he was officially declared mentally ill. Political madness and mental illness were indistinguishable to the All-Union Society of Psychiatrists. When Semyon Gluzman, an accredited psychiatrist, wrote a dissenting opinion, it was officially self-evident that he too was suffering from deviance. For his efforts, he was sentenced to ten years in labor camp and exile.

Reddaway detailed the process of discovery that led from illicit expert examinations by independent psychiatrists who took great personal risk, to the confirming investigation by international experts in 1989. The All-Union Society had sought to preempt expulsion from the World Psychiatric Association (WPA) by withdrawing in 1983. The investigatory commission set medical and ethical conditions for the return of the discredited Soviet society to the WPA. An important step was taken when Tatyana Dmitrieva, chairman of Moscow's Serbsky Institute on Forensic Psychiatry, confirmed in the *Psychiatric News* of July 17, 1992, that psychiatric abuse was systemic in the Soviet Union. Reddaway pointed out that this revelation was published only in the *Psychiatric News*. He expressed the hope that Soviet and other publications would follow suit. Reddaway suggested that Memorial try to uncover more of this history through its investigations in the KGB archives as well as through its oral history research.

A former Polish dissident, Marek Karpinsky, described the influence of the Russian dissident movement on the Polish dissident movement. He illustrated his point with an anecdote about how, when he and Adam Michnik were arrested in January 1968, they sat in jail together and sang Russian protest songs because there weren't any Polish ones! That was during what he termed the "first wave." By the time of the "second wave," Polish underground literature and sentiment had become very anti-Soviet. Karpinsky joked that by that time there were Polish songs aplenty to sing in jail.

Mid-way through the conference, Memorial organized a computer evening program to illustrate how the data on victims were being processed. Long sheets of impersonal computer printouts, recording in deceptively dry detail the unspeakable fate of victims of repression, were circulated to the audience. It was a necessary and essential, but also jarring, routinization of personal tragedy. The data were arranged systematically— date of arrest, article of the Criminal Code, place of imprisonment, sentence, and so forth. Other data were arranged thematically according to biographical information. Both the value of having this information stored in computer systems and the access that this permits were apparent to visitors.

Focusing on the current struggle to reclaim national identity, Yevgeny Zakharov of the Kharkov Memorial discussed the history of the Ukrainian movement for national realization. He stated that in the period under investigation, arrests were made in more than 1,000 municipalities on the basis of Ukrainian self-nationalization. Many were sent to the Mordovian camps. The Ukrainian Memorial chapters are researching the Ukrainian opposition movement.

During the morning of the final day, members of Memorial's Scientific Research Center (NITS) presented a detailed account of their research in the KGB archives. Nikita Petrov outlined the structure of the KGB, describing the historical function of a number of its sub-units and their role in the struggle with dissidence. Arseny Roginsky, whose archive odyssey a decade earlier we have previously noted, compared the work in the KGB archives to the tasks of 17th century historians trying to analyze *letopisi* (ancient church chronicles). He explained that a methodology for analyzing these archives and establishing the validity of particular documents had not yet been developed.

In their presentation, Arseny Roginsky and Nikita Okhotin touched upon the issue of quantifying the dissident movement and the number of people arrested on political articles. They were able to provide some figures on arrests and convictions on anti-Soviet articles; for example, from 1967 to 1975 1,583 people were convicted on articles 70 (anti-Soviet agitation and propaganda) and 190-1 (wittingly disseminating fabrications discrediting the Soviet political and social system, an article introduced to the RSFSR Criminal Code in 1966). In the preceeding decade (1958–1966) a total of 3,448 people were convicted for anti-Soviet agitation and propaganda. In the year 1958 alone, a time often referred to in the West as a "period of liberalization," 1,416 people were arrested and convicted on article 70 (or 58–10, its predecessor)! As many as 6,000 arrests were made between 1958 and 1986 on these political articles.[3] To better understand these statistics we need only recall the official ambivalence of the "de-Stalinization" campaign that began under Khrushchev (see chapter 3). Another statistic they presented showed that in 1976 13 percent of those who were discovered to be authors of anonymous anti-Soviet texts (leaflets, brochures, letters) were labelled "mentally ill,"[4] a clear indication of the extent to which psychiatry had been subverted in the struggle to suppress dissidents. As the Communist Party grew in power, it subsumed more and more individual rights. Dissidence was prima facie evidence of either treason or mental illness. Even potential dissidence, for example, occupying a position of leadership in a national or religious organization or authoring pamphlets, became grounds for prophylactic arrests. Telephone taps and censorship of correspondence were a routine part of state surveillance.

Despite the amount of information becoming available to researchers, Roginsky asserted that statistics remain one of the most inaccessible areas of information. Between bureaucratic obstacles and documents that were destroyed, Memorial is not passively waiting until all the numbers become available. It is actively employing questionnaires to feed responses into a database.

The closing discussion returned to the theme of defining dissidence. Larisa Bogoraz challenged the audience, stating that there had been 270 million dissidents—encompassing the entire population of a country enveloped in a mad system. Others restricted the designation of dissidents to those who realized that the myth of unity was indeed a myth. Daniel asserted that society itself should be the object of study along with the leadership's ability to govern it. The nature of social conformity and nonconformity as well as various forms of protest should be examined. Oral history should be recorded and analyzed in order to understand dissidence. Daniel anticipated that new literature based on letters, memoirs and "mountains" of testimony would be created in the coming years.

Attuned as the participants were to the issues of continuity and change in Soviet political and social life, the most immediately evident change was that this was the first international conference on the hitherto forbidden theme to take place in Russia. Previous meetings had to be held in Western locations such as London and New York. Also of great importance to Memorial was the fact that foreign specialists came to the conference. Daniel stressed the point that the cooperation and assistance of international scholars in this field has helped and continues to help Memorial to develop.

Memorial has come a long way since the 1987 signature-gathering campaign. It is difficult to make a definitive statement about Memorial's character and activities because the organization continues to evolve. Regarding its significance in a particular period, this examination of Memorial has focused on the organization's development from its inception until the dissolution of the Soviet Union. The explicit themes of the August 1992 international conference on dissidence were those of identity, origins and new directions; the implicit theme was the triumphant celebration of a movement that had survived against all odds. The gathering, with its deliberations on historical themes and *past-tense* review of dissidence, attested to a perhaps fleeting moment of reflection and stability for Memorial, whose course will depend on the unfolding events in what was once called the Soviet Union.

NOTES

1. William Faulkner used this phrase about mankind when he accepted the Nobel Prize for literature.

2. Vladimir Pribylovsky, *Slovar Novykh Politicheskykh Partii i Organizatii Rossii (Dictionary of New Political Parties and Organizations in Russia)*, Information Group "Panorama," Moscow, November 1991, p. 40.

3. Arseny Roginsky, Nikita Okhotin, "About Various Sources on the History of the Dissident Movement," speech, Moscow, August 26, 1992.

4. In general, diagnoses of "mental illness" required "treatment" in Ordinary or Special Psychiatric Hospitals.

Appendix A

In their 1989 book entitled *What Happened in That Time?*, historians L. A. Gordon and E. V. Klopov conclude that between 1931 and 1936 no less than 4 to 5 million lives were lost as a result of hunger and repression (pp. 162–163), and in the second half of the 1930s through the beginning of the 1940s, as many as 4 million died by execution. The official historian, D. A. Volkogonov, estimates (based on inconclusive information) that in the years 1937–1939 alone, 3.5 to 4 million were "repressed" (*Oktyabr*, no. 12, 1988, p. 129); V. Danilov attributes as many as 6 to 7 million deaths between 1931 and 1933 to famine alone ("Fenomen pervykh pyatiletok," *Gorizont*, no. 5, 1988, p. 35). V. V. Tsaplin, basing his analysis on documents from the State Central Economic Administration, arrived at an (inconclusive) total of 7.9 million people who died of hunger or in prisons and camps between the years 1927 and 1938, while another 2 million left the Soviet Union ("Statistika zhertv stalinizma v 30–e gg.," *Voprosi Istorii*, no. 4, 1989, pp. 175–181). V. Chistyakovoy asserts that in the year 1933 as many as 5 million people died of hunger and illness. Furthermore, he estimates that between 1936 and 1950 up to 12 million prisoners were being held in camps annually, in total 12 million died. This latter figure includes those who were executed as well as victims of postwar repression. Finally, he concludes that 20 million Soviet citizens became victims in the 1930s (V. Chistyakovoy, *Neva*, no. 10, 1988, pp. 154, 158). In *Let History Judge*, Roy Medvedev asserts that between 1937 and 1938 one thousand people were executed daily *in Moscow alone* (*Kotlovan, Spetsialny Vypusk, Khibinskogo otdeleniya obshchestva "Memorial"*).

Some researchers have arrived at even more shocking figures: a candidate in physics and mathematics, I. G. Dyadkin, in an article entitled "Demographic Statistics of Unnatural Deaths in the USSR (1918–1956)," says the number was 56 to 62 million! Interestingly, he asserts that there were three times as many victims (9 million) from the 1918–1923 Civil War's terror, famine and disease than in the 1937–1940 period (3–3.4 million), which included the Finnish War. If such figures are accurate, then the major elements of what is called Stalinism were very clearly manifested in the early years of Lenin's leadership. Dyadkin estimates that 13 to 15 million died between 1929 and 1936 and 21 to 34 million died in the war or from repression between 1941 and 1949 ("Demograficheskaya statistika neyestestvennoy smertnosti v SSSR, 1918–1956)," *Referendum*, no. 29–30, 18 March–15 April, 1989, Moscow Samizdat). The American historian John Gold arrived at a total figure of 50 to 60 million victims (*Kotlovan*, ibid.).

Appendix B

Confirmed by the Founding Conference
of the All-Union voluntary
historical-enlightenment society
"Memorial"
January 28, 1989

CHARTER

of the All-Union voluntary
historical-enlightenment society
"MEMORIAL"

1. GENERAL PROVISIONS

1.1. The All-Union voluntary historical-enlightenment society "Memorial" (from here on the Society "Memorial"), based on the federated principle of structure, is a public organization carrying out its activities in accordance with the Constitution of the USSR, the legislation of the Union of SSR, union and autonomous republics, the international legal obligations of the USSR, and also the present Charter.

Members of the Society "Memorial" unite in their humanistic moral principles, objection to lawlessness, discrimination, violation of the rights of individuals and peoples, aspiration to enable the formation of civic virtues in the Soviet people, condemnation of arbitrariness and force as a means of solving social problems and social conflicts.

1.2. The Society "Memorial's" founders are: an initiative group of citizens as well as the Union of Architects of the USSR, the Union of Designers of the USSR, the Cinematographers Union of the USSR, *Literaturnaya Gazeta*, the magazine *Ogonyok*, the Union of Theatrical Figures of the USSR, the Union of Artists of the USSR.

1.3. The Society "Memorial" consists of local divisions and other forms of organization (from here on—local societies), acting on the principles of autonomy and self-governance. A central elected organ of the Society "Memorial" (Administrative Board) is created for the coordination of activities of local societies. The Board's authority is determined by the present Charter.

The realm of activities of local societies might not coincide with existing administrative-territorial divisions.

Local societies have the right to any form of association and coordination within the Society "Memorial," including that they may unite in republic and interrepublic formation and create corresponding coordinating electoral organs.

The Foundation "Memorial" is part of the structure of the Society "Memorial." The Social Council of the Foundation "Memorial" manages the means of the Foundation "Memorial."

Local societies, the Leadership and the foundation "Memorial" are juridical entities and have independent bank accounts.

1.4. The Society "Memorial" is active in all the territories of the USSR.

1.5. The Society "Memorial" carries out its activities in cooperation with state, public, religious organizations and democratic movements in the USSR, foreign international organizations and foundations whose goals and activities do not contradict the goals and principles of the Society "Memorial." Organizations wishing to contribute to and take part in the activities of the Society "Memorial" may enter in the capacity of member-trustees.

2. THE GOALS AND FORMS OF ACTIVITY OF THE SOCIETY "MEMORIAL"

2.1. The Society "Memorial" sets the following goals for itself:

a) the preservation and immortalization of the memory of victims of Stalinism;

b) rendering help unto those who suffered from repression, and the creation of their associations; comprehensive defense of their legal interests in all state and public institutions; activities directed at the adoption of state measures for compensation to those who had damage (repression) inflicted upon them and granting them immediate social welfare;

c) the creation in the city of Moscow with the means of the foundation "Memorial" of a Memorial complex including a monument to the victims of Stalinism, and also a scientific-information and enlightenment center with a publicly accessible archive, museum and library, materials that contain information on the repressions of Stalinism;

d) the creation in the territory of the USSR of other memorial complexes and monuments to the victims of repressions;

e) the restoration of the historical truth on the crimes of Stalinism, on illegal and terrorist methods of governing, the study of their cause and consequence; assistance in the acknowledgment of crimes of Stalinism as crimes against humanity; close cooperation with the Commission of the Politburo of the Central Committee of the Communist Party of the Soviet Union on the supplementary study of materials connected with repressions that took place in the period of the 1930s and 1940s and in the beginning of the 1950s; close cooperation with the commissions under the Congress of People's Deputies created for rendering help to Soviet organs in securing the rights and interests of those who are rehabilitated, the creation of monuments to the victims of repression and the maintenance of their place of burial in a fitting manner, and other state and public commissions doing the same kinds of activities.

f) assistance in the complete and open rehabilitation of the victims of repression;

g) active participation in democratic transformations, assistance in the development of civic and legal consciousness in fellow citizens, struggle against illegal acts, education of the younger generation in the spirit of a legal government.

2.2. In order to carry out the Charter's goals, the Society is conducting the following activities:

a) forms public opinion on the resolving of charter tasks of the Society by way of publicized speeches, lectures, the collection of voluntary contributions, the collection of signatures under petitions and other legal methods;

b) collects, acquires, processes and preserves information as well as material relics and valuables connected with the facts and circumstances of repression and events accompanying it;

c) assists in the opening of access to sources of information (archives, libraries and museum foundations, etc.), publishes books, documents and materials on the subject of the activities of the Society; conducts lectures, debates, exhibitions; announces competitions and so forth.

d) publishes a periodical information bulletin on its activities.

3. MEMBERS OF THE SOCIETY "MEMORIAL"

3.1. Membership in the Society "Memorial" may be individual or individual and collective by discretion of local societies. The rights and duties of collective members are determined by local societies. In voting, one collective member of the Society "Memorial" has one vote.

3.2. Individuals or organizations who share the goals of the Society, who accept its charter and participate in its activities, may be members of the Society "Memorial."

Membership in the Society "Memorial" is incompatible with propaganda or the practices of national or religious intolerance, anti-humanist ideas.

3.3. Individual members of the Society "Memorial" have the right to vote and be elected to all organs of the Society.

Members of the Society "Memorial" occupying staff positions in the apparatus of the Society may not be elected to the central organs of the Society.

3.4. Acceptance of individual citizens and organizations as members of the Society "Memorial" is carried out by the local societies.

The Board may admit from five (in rural areas) to ten citizens as individual members of the Society "Memorial" according to their collective statements.

3.5. Cessation of membership in the Society "Memorial" comes about as a result of:

a) declaration of a member of the Society;

b) decision of a local society taken in connection with violation of the Charter by a member of the Society "Memorial."

3.6. The necessity of admission and membership dues, the custom and periodicalness of their payment are determined by local societies. Members of the Society "Memorial" who were subjected to repression are exempt from paying dues.

4. CENTRAL ORGANS OF THE SOCIETY "MEMORIAL"

4.1. The central organs of the Society "Memorial" are:
a) The Conference;

b) The Social Council of the Foundation "Memorial";

c) The Administrative Board and its Work group;

d) The Revision commission;

4.2. The Conference is the highest organ of the Society "Memorial." The next conference is summoned by the Board of the Society not less than once in three years. Delegates of local societies and unions of the repressed, members of the Social Council of the Foundation "Memorial," representatives of the organizational-founders of the All-Union Society Memorial participate in the work of the Conference as voting members. The norms of representation and the custom of choosing delegates is determined by the Board of the Society "Memorial."

The Conference adopts the Charter of the Society "Memorial" and introduces changes in it; confirms the basic directions of the activities of the Board and its budget; hears and confirms reports of the Board and the Revision Commission; elects members of the Board who are not delegates to the Board from local societies and unions of the repressed; elects members of the Work group, co-chairmen of the Board, members of the Revision commission and other elective organs of the Society "Memorial."

Decisions of the Conference are taken by a simple majority of votes with the presence of not less than half of the voting delegates elected there. The manner of voting is determined by the Conference.

The Board of the Society "Memorial" calls the next Conference on the request of not less than one-third of local societies, on the request of the Social Council or on its own initiative. In the case of unfulfilled requests of the local societies or Social Council they themselves create an Organizational Committee, which calls an extraordinary Conference.

4.3. The Social Council of the Foundation "Memorial," chosen according to the results of a survey of the population from prominent social figures—active and consequent fighters for democracy and glasnost, and for the irreversibility of the processes of perestroika—is confirmed by the Conference of the Society "Memorial."

The Social Council checks the work of the Board of the Society "Memorial," confirms the estimates of expenditures on the construction and activity of the Memorial Complex in Moscow in agreement with the Charter of the foundation "Memorial," as well as programs of work of the scientific-information and enlightenment center of the Memorial Complex.

4.4. The Board of the Society "Memorial" is formed:

a) from representatives of local societies, who are delegated by the latter to the Board;

b) from representatives of unions of the repressed, who are delegated by them to the Board;

c) from representatives of the organizational-founders of the All-Union Society "Memorial" (there is one representative in the Board from each of these organizational-founders of the Society "Memorial");

d) from members who are elected to the Conference from the members of the Society "Memorial."

The standards of representation of local societies and unions of the repressed in the Board and the amount of members in the Board who are chosen by the Conference on a personal basis is determined by the Conference. The Board, its co-chairmen and the Work group of the Board are chosen in the period between conferences.

The Board works out plans of its work and budget, presents them for confirmation of the Conference and gives an account to the Conference of their fulfillment. The Board assists in the exchange of information and materials between local societies and between them and the scientific-information and enlightenment center of the Memorial Complex in Moscow as well as assisting in the circulation of textual, photo-movie-video and other materials, which are located with local societies.

The Board coordinates the work of local societies, calls the regular and extraordinary conferences of the Society "Memorial."

In the case of a discrepancy in the activities of local societies with the Charter of the Society "Memorial," the Board has the right to suspend the membership of the local society in the Society "Memorial" right up to the decision of the Conference.

The Board has a self-sufficient balance. The manager of credits is determined by the Board. Local societies do not carry the responsibility for the financial obligations of the Board. For resolving the tasks of the Society "Memorial" the Board has the right to create enterprises including publishing ones.

The Board registers local societies and distributes to them corresponding documents of the Society "Memorial."

The Board registers member-trustees of the Society "Memorial."

Meetings of the Board are conducted not less than two times a year. Decisions of the Board are taken by simple majority vote and are authorized when not less than half of the members of the Board participate in the vote.

All meetings of the Board are open. The times for meetings (plenums) of the Board and the agenda of local societies, unions of the repressed, elective organs of the Society and organizational-founders of the Society "Memorial" are to be informed not less than a month in advance. The minutes of all meetings are kept. The minutes of the meetings and all other documents of the Board and all central organs of the Society "Memorial" are kept in the archive of the Society "Memorial" and are presented to any member of the Society "Memorial" on his request. The decisions of the meetings (plenums) of the Board are sent to all local societies and organizational-founders of the Society "Memorial." The activity of the Board and local societies is regularly brought to light in the information bulletin of the Society "Memorial."

4.5. A Work group of the Board is elected by the Conference for the conducting of the current work of the Society "Memorial" from the members of the Board. The number of members of the Work group is determined by the Conference. The Work group is accountable to the Board of the Society "Memorial."

Any member of the Board of the Society "Memorial" has the right to participate in the Work group as a voting member.

4.6. Co-chairmen of the Board of the Society "Memorial" are directed in their activities by the decisions of the Conference and the Board and regularly account their activities at meetings of the Board of the Society "Memorial."

4.7. The Revision Commission of the Society "Memorial" checks the administrative and financial activity of the Board of the Society "Memorial," the composition and account of the material value that is on the balance of the Society "Memorial," and gives an account of the results of its activities to the Conference. The Revision Commission functions on the basis of the Regulation on the Revision Commission, confirmed by the Conference. The chairman of the Revision Commission takes part in the work of the Board as a non-voting member.

5. LOCAL SOCIETIES

5.1. Members of the Society "Memorial" (numbering not less than ten, in rural localities, five) may create local societies.

5.2. The establishment of local societies is registered by the Board of the Society "Memorial," in a month's time in which they distribute corresponding documents to local societies. The Board is obligated to register a local society if its establishment occurred in accordance with the Charter of the Society "Memorial." The local society registered by the Board, is a juridical entity that independently disposes of its financial means and determines the management of credits.

5.3. The local society, as a juridical entity, has an independent balance and account. For the solving of its problems the local society may create enterprises, including publishing ones. The local society may independently be occupied with foreign economic activity.

The Board of the Society does not bear responsibility for the financial obligations of local societies, and local societies do not bear responsibility for the financial obligations of the Board and each other.

5.4. Local societies are, within the framework of the Charter of the Society "Memorial," free to choose the form and methods of their activities, and also in questions of their internal structure.

5.5. Local societies do not have the right to represent the Society "Memorial" unless it is either in the framework of the general program of the Society "Memorial" or the decision of the Conference of the Society "Memorial."

6. FINANCIAL MEANS OF THE SOCIETY AND THE FOUNDATION "MEMORIAL"

6.1. The financial means of the Society "Memorial" and the Foundation "Memorial" are made up of:

a) voluntary contributions, donations, bequests and other payments of citizens, institutions, enterprises and organizations in the USSR and abroad;

b) the income from publishing, lecture and other charter activities of the Society "Memorial" as well as receipts from concerts, evenings and other measures carried out in the Society or the foundation "Memorial's" favor;

c) special state subsidies.

The financial means of the Society "Memorial" are also made up of:

—introductory and membership dues,

—deductions of the organizational-founders.

6.2. The Board of the Society "Memorial" has an account in the Zhilsotzbank of the USSR and also a hard currency account in the Vneshekonombank of the USSR.

6.3. The means in the foundation "Memorial" go to account no. 700454 in the Zhilsotzbank of the USSR as well as to account no. 70000005 V/O Soyuz-sovrazchot in the Vneshekonombank of the USSR.

6.4. The financing of various programs of the Society "Memorial" or joint initiatives of local societies as well as the distribution of income from this activity happen on the basis of agreements, the supporters of which may be local societies, the Board, the Foundation "Memorial," the enterprise of the Society "Memorial" as well as supportive organizations, including foreign ones.

6.5. The Society "Memorial," its local societies and enterprises as well as the Foundation "Memorial" are free from paying taxes, state duties, customs and other collections, which are entered in the state budget of the USSR.

7. THE LEGAL SITUATION OF THE SOCIETY "MEMORIAL"

7.1. The Board of the Society "Memorial," the Foundation "Memorial," local societies are juridical entities and do not bear responsibility for the obligations of one another.

7.2. The Board of the Society "Memorial," the foundation "Memorial," local societies have a stamp and seal of their names. A Society may have its own emblems and signs.

7.3. The Society "Memorial" may be liquidated by decision of the Conference, qualified by a majority of two-thirds of the votes. The Conference after satisfying legal pretenses decides the question of its property in accordance with legislation currently in force.

7.4. The location of the central organs of the Society "Memorial" is the city of Moscow.

Text collated with the documents of the Editorial commission and a shorthand of the meeting of the Conference of January 28, 1989.

Chairman of the editorial commission: G. C. Lebedev, Leningrad

Members of the commission:

E. M. Ametistov, Moscow
L. D. Batkin, Moscow
A. A. Deko, Kiev
P. R. Zenkyevich, Moscow
B. A. Israyelson, Leningrad
A. A. Kovalyev, Leningrad
V. V. Kurochkin, Chita
O. E. Lipikhin, Omsk
D. I. Musatov, Riga
G. Y. Rakitskaya, Moscow
V. A. Semenyov, Syktyvkar
L. S. Trus, Novosibirsk

C. B. Sheboldaev, Moscow
Y. P. Shchekochikhin, Moscow
M. N. Yukhma, Cheboksary

NOTE

The post-Soviet Memorial Charter is entitled "CHARTER of the historical-enlightenment, charitable and human rights society 'Memorial'." It defines the Society Memorial as "a union of self-governing societies, foundations and other types of organizations as well as individuals that share the goals and tasks stipulated in the present Charter and act in accordance with the legislation of their countries and their own Charters." In the new Charter, all references relating to the specifics of the Soviet situation have been omitted for at least two reasons. First, because the Soviet Union no longer exists, its structure, constitution, and legislation do not have to be addressed. Second, some of Memorial's goals relating to Stalinism, for example, the erection of a monument to its victims in Moscow, have already been achieved. The new Charter of Memorial places the former Soviet Society's aims and tasks in a broader, global context; Memorial's status is now that of an international organization. Its goals have shifted from the struggle against Stalinism to challenging international totalitarianism. It seeks, for example, the restoration of the historical truth and the immortalization of the memory of all "victims of political repressions" (the original Charter refers to "victims of crimes of Stalinism"). An addition to the legal status section states that Memorial may act as plaintiff and defendant in a court of arbitration in order to fulfill the Charter's goals and the tasks of the Society. Time will tell whether this larger mandate will seek trials of those guilty of crimes of totalitarianism.

Selected Bibliography

Bialer, Seweryn. *Stalin's Successors*. Cambridge: Cambridge University Press, 1980.

Conquest, Robert. *The Great Terror: Stalin's Purges of the Thirties*. Middlesex, England: Penguin Books, 1968.

Heller, Michel, and Nekrich, Aleksandr. *Utopia in Power*.London: Hutchinson, 1986.

Gorbatschows historische Rede. Munich: Wilhelm Heyne Verlag, 1987.

Laqueur, Walter. *Stalin: The Glasnost Revelations*. New York: Charles Scribner's Sons, 1990.

Medvedev, Roy. *Let History Judge*. New York: Alfred A. Knopf, 1971.

Nove, Alec. *Glasnost in Action*. Boston: Unwin Hyman, 1989.

Nyeformaly: Civil Society in the USSR. A Helsinki Watch Report. New York: Helsinki Watch, February 1990.

Rubenstein, Joshua. *Soviet Dissidents: Their Struggle for Human Rights*. Boston: Beacon Press, 1980.

Tucker, Robert C., ed. *Stalinism: Essays in Historical Interpretation*. New York: W. W. Norton & Company, 1977.

Index

About the Author

NANCI ADLER, a graduate of Columbia University and the University of Amsterdam (the Netherlands), is with the Geneva Initiative on Psychiatry and the Second World Center in Amsterdam. She is a contributor to numerous journals.